Contents

How to use this book   v

Part 1: The Learning Curve

Introduction to IT and ICT   2
Hardware and software   5
Using databases   12
Using the Internet   16
Spreadsheets   22
Word processors   27
Graphics   33
Communicating   35
Glossary   40

Part 2: The Bottom Line

What the unit expects   44
Evidence for level 3   46
Other forms of assessment and evidence   55

Part 3: Opportunities

Evidence from A-level courses   58
Art • Biology • Business Studies • Chemistry • Computing • Design and Technology • General Studies • Geography • History • Mathematics • Physics

Evidence from Vocational A-Level courses   86
Art and Design • Business • Construction and the Built Environment • Engineering • Health and Social Care • Hospitality and Catering • Information and Communication Technology • Land and Environment • Leisure and Recreation • Manufacturing • Media: Communication and Production • Performing Arts • Retail and Distributive Services • Science • Travel and Tourism

Information sources   118

Index   127

How to use this book

This book helps you obtain the key skill called Information Technology level 3. You will be doing your key skills with your other studies in a school, college or at work. The common combinations are:

Level 3
A-level and key skills
Vocational A-level and key skills

An Information Technology key skill is not asking you to be a computer expert. It is about knowing some facts about modern information systems and communication technology and showing that you can actually use them in real life. Most of us need a reminder about how to use IT and this book is organised to provide rapid help when you want it.

The good news about gaining any of the key skills is that you don't always need to do extra work. The evidence for the key skill is produced while you are doing your normal study and work such as in the classroom, laboratory, workshop, or while working at a job.

Of course there is a certain cunning in knowing which of your work to keep and how to show it, and that's what this book is about. There are special sections for all popular A-level and Vocational A-Level subjects which tell you exactly what you need to do.

You can use this book in different ways; it depends on what you need. For example, you might not need to read it from the beginning. To get the most out of this book, have a look at the following summary of how it is organised and decide how you can use it best.

The GNVQ Advanced awards are now called **Vocational A-levels**.

From September 2001 GNVQ Foundation and Intermediate awards are likely to be known as **Vocational GCSEs**.

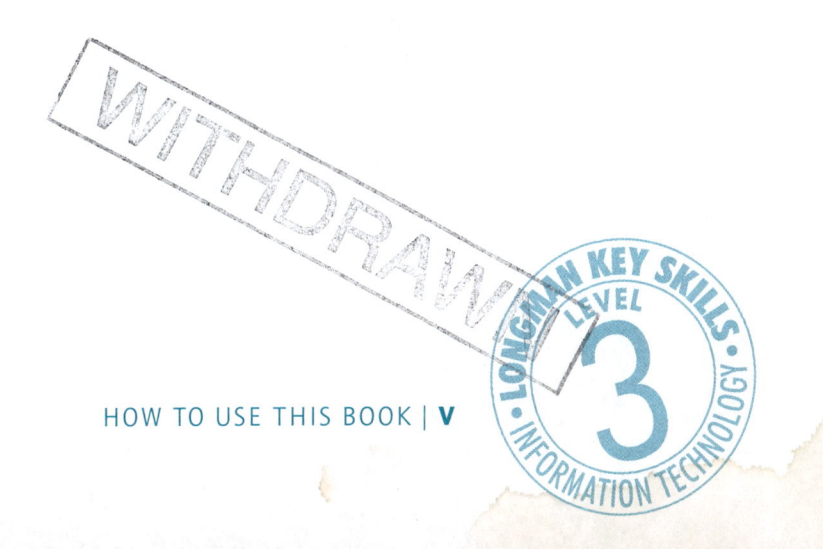

Part 1: The Learning Curve

This part of the book concentrates on what you need to know to get the key skill units. It has useful information about computers and the Internet, and how to use word processing, database, spreadsheet and graphics programs. It concentrates on the more tricky ideas and has clear worked examples to show you how to use them.

You can check that you have the basic knowledge needed by the key skill units. If you are up to speed with your IT then you may not need much of this section.

Part 2: The Bottom Line

This part of the book tells you what you must do to gain the key skills units. It explains:

- The words and ideas of the key skills
- The definition of level 3
- How you can practise the skills
- What must be in your portfolio of evidence

Your collection of evidence or portfolio is the key to getting your key skill. This part of the book tells you how to choose your evidence and get it ready.

Part 3: Opportunities

This part of the book tells you where to find opportunities for evidence in the study or work you are already doing. If you are at school or college, you should look up the pages for your particular subjects at A-level or Vocational A-Level.

Everyone can make a start on using IT to find information by looking at the chapter on **Information sources**. It lists some useful and interesting website addresses.

Margin

Look in the margin for simple explanations of important words and ideas and for references to other places in the book where there is useful information.

Part 1: The Learning Curve

This part concentrates on what you need to know to get your key skills qualification. It will show you:

- How to use computers and the Internet in practical situations.
- Techniques for getting the most of out word processing, database, spreadsheet and graphics programs.
- Clear explanations of the more difficult ideas.

This part is divided into nine sections:

- **Introduction to IT and ICT**
- **Hardware and software**
- **Databases**
- **Using the Internet**
- **Spreadsheets**
- **Word processors**
- **Graphics**
- **Communicating**
- **Glossary**

Introduction to IT and ICT

Examples of IT/ICT
computers
email
Webpages
mobile phones
phone services
CD-ROMs
digital TV
teletext
videoconferencing
cash dispensers
smart tills

IT is shorthand for information technology. The alternate abbreviation ICT is shorthand for information and communications technology.

Although computers are an important part of information technology, there are many other forms of IT. You are using IT when you use a phone with memory buttons, when you program your video recorder, when you withdraw money from an automatic cash dispenser, or shop at a store with a barcode reader.

This part concentrates on areas of IT where people often need help, especially when using computer software. The content is not very technical but you may have to learn some new ideas which will help you to make better use of your IT. Some of the ideas have their own special words; these words are often placed in the margin, alongside a relevant section. At any time you can also look up words in the glossary on page 40.

How IT can help you

Information technology helps our lives in many ways; here are some examples:

- New types of job, e.g. working at home
- New types of business, e.g. business on the Internet
- New ways of getting information, e.g. travel timetables
- New ways of messaging people, e.g. email and mobile phones
- New ways of shopping, e.g. e-commerce
- New ways of paying, e.g. electronic money

As you use IT for your various tasks you also need to be able to think about how you might have done it without IT, or if it was possible without IT.

Effects of IT

Using IT makes our lives easier but some of the advantages go hand in hand with possible disadvantages. Some common uses of IT are listed in the table, and you should at least know a few issues associated with using

IT. When thinking about advantages and disadvantages of IT you should always:

- Keep an open mind about benefits and drawbacks
- Concentrate on facts not opinion

IT effect	Some advantages	Some disadvantages
Job changes	New jobs are created Existing jobs are more interesting People can work from home without travel	Loss of old jobs Possible health hazards from using IT equipment Loss of contact with people at work
Electronic money EFTPOS (electronic funds transfer at point of sale) (e.g. swipe cards)	Security from theft Quicker transfer between accounts Faster turnover at checkouts Better flow of goods to the shelves	You need a bank account Not suitable for small items There may be charges Possible stress on shop assistants Difficult for small shops
IT in and between banks EFT (electronic funds transfer)	Security from theft Quicker transfer between bank accounts	You need a bank account Not suitable for small items There may be charges
E-commerce (e.g. shopping on the Internet)	You can order from anywhere in the world Prices are competitive	Someone still has to deliver goods to your home
IT used for information systems in shops and factories	Automatic ordering of stock and parts Saves doing boring and repetitive jobs	Loss of old jobs Possible health hazards from using IT equipment
Communications	Rapid email to anywhere in the world Targeting mail to particular names and addresses	Possible loss of privacy
Private life	Easier to get information Easier shopping Cheaper quotes for travel and other services Possible new jobs	Loss of privacy Feelings of increased pressure

Protection of rights

Data protection

At some stage most of us get advertising information mailed out by a system which has our personal details on an IT database. Our personal

INTRODUCTION TO IT AND ICT | 3

Personal data
date of birth
phone number
income
health record

details, such as age or phone number, are often collected by organisations who then store the information. There are regulations designed to protect us against any misuse of this data. It is legal for companies to hold personal data on their database provided they have registered under the **Data Protection Act**, but this personal data is not allowed to be published or used unless you give permission.

Copyright

Other information is subject to the various laws of copyright. Copyright allows artists or authors to own the way that their original work appears. You need to remember copyright if you want to copy and use other people's text or graphics in your own work. The safest way to operate is to use material which you know is free of copyright. There are Internet sites where you can copy clip art that is free of copyright.

Hardware and software

This chapter tells you, or reminds you, about the basic technology of computers and their use.

- Components of computer systems
- User interfaces and operating systems
- Features for editing work
- Directory and file structures
- Advanced program features

Components of a computer

A computer is a machine which can automatically take in data, process data and output the results. It does this by following a set of instructions called a **program**. Modern digital computers can be grouped in the following forms:

- **Mainframe computer:** a powerful computer with many input and output devices. Banks use mainframes.
- **Minicomputer:** a compact but powerful computer with many input and output devices. Superstores use minis.
- **Personal computer:** a small computer with a microprocessor intended for use by one person. Homes and offices use PCs.
- **Microprocessor:** an integrated circuit which contains the processor part of a computer on one chip. TVs use microprocessors.

All computers have parts which are either hardware or software:

- **Hardware** is the computer equipment.
- **Software** is the set of programs which tell the computer what to do, such as run a game or be a word processor.

The computer reads and uses software programs stored on magnetic disks, on CD-ROMs or in other computers connected by networks.

Computer interfaces

When working with computers you need an interface so that you can put information in and get information back. The common types of interface on a personal computer are:

Analogue data can be represented by a voltage that varies, constantly getting bigger or smaller.

Digital data can be represented by a voltage that is either high or low (1 or 0).

Hardware
processor (CPU)
memory (RAM)
disk storage
screen (VDU)
keyboard
mouse, joystick
printer, plotter

Software
Windows program
word processor programs
CAD programs
games programs

> **TYPES OF COMPUTER DISK**
>
> - Hard disks are sealed inside the computer.
> - Floppy disks can be removed by the user.
> - CD-ROMs can also be removed by the user.
>
> *Note*: The spelling is **disk** not **disc**.

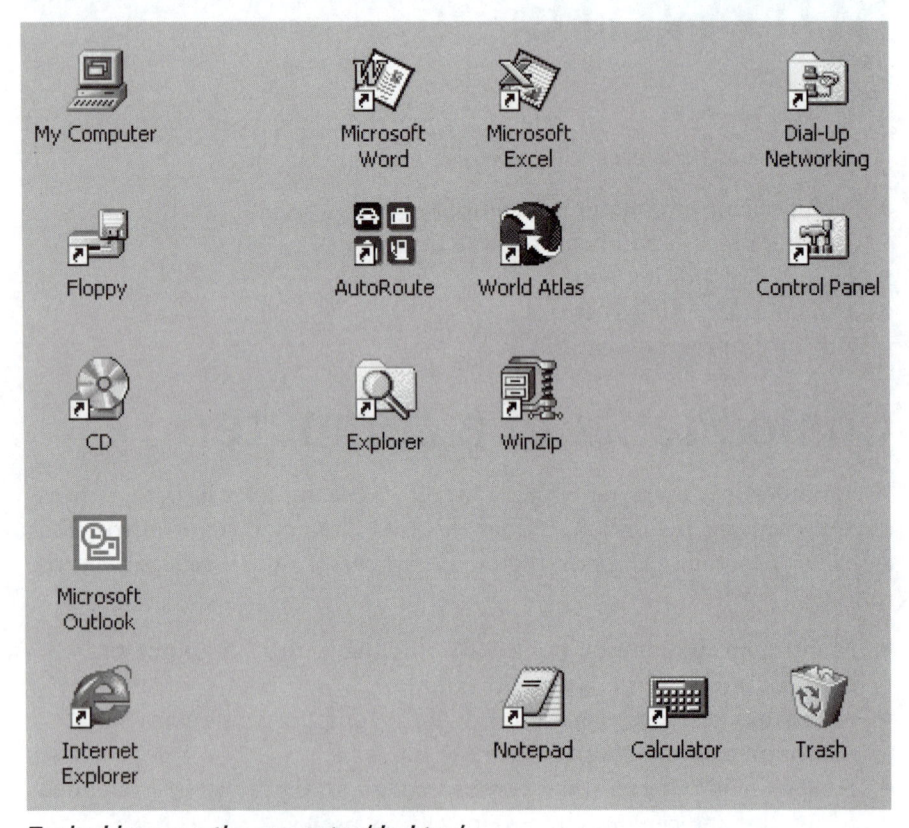

Typical icons on the computer 'desktop'

An **icon** is a small picture used instead of words; clicking on an icon usually starts an activity.

- **Input:** keyboard, mouse
- **Output:** screen, printer

You operate the inputs and outputs with the help of an operating system and interface program such as **Windows**. There are other operating systems, e.g. Mac OS, Unix and Linux. A graphical interface, like the Windows interface or the Mac OS interface, uses icons; selecting the appropriate icon will start a program or open a document.

Editing

All programs allow you to edit and make changes on-screen. Clicking on the **Edit** group of the menu bar at the top of the screen gives a drop-down menu with the available editing options. Here are some commonly used functions:

- **Cut** deletes but keeps an invisible copy.
- **Copy** leaves the original untouched but makes a copy.
- **Paste** produces a copy at the cursor position.

As you get more experienced, you might notice the shortcuts given alongside the edit commands. For example, the shortcut for **Cut** is **Ctrl-C**, which means hold the Ctrl key down and press C.

Highlight your choice then...

Cut

Copy

Paste

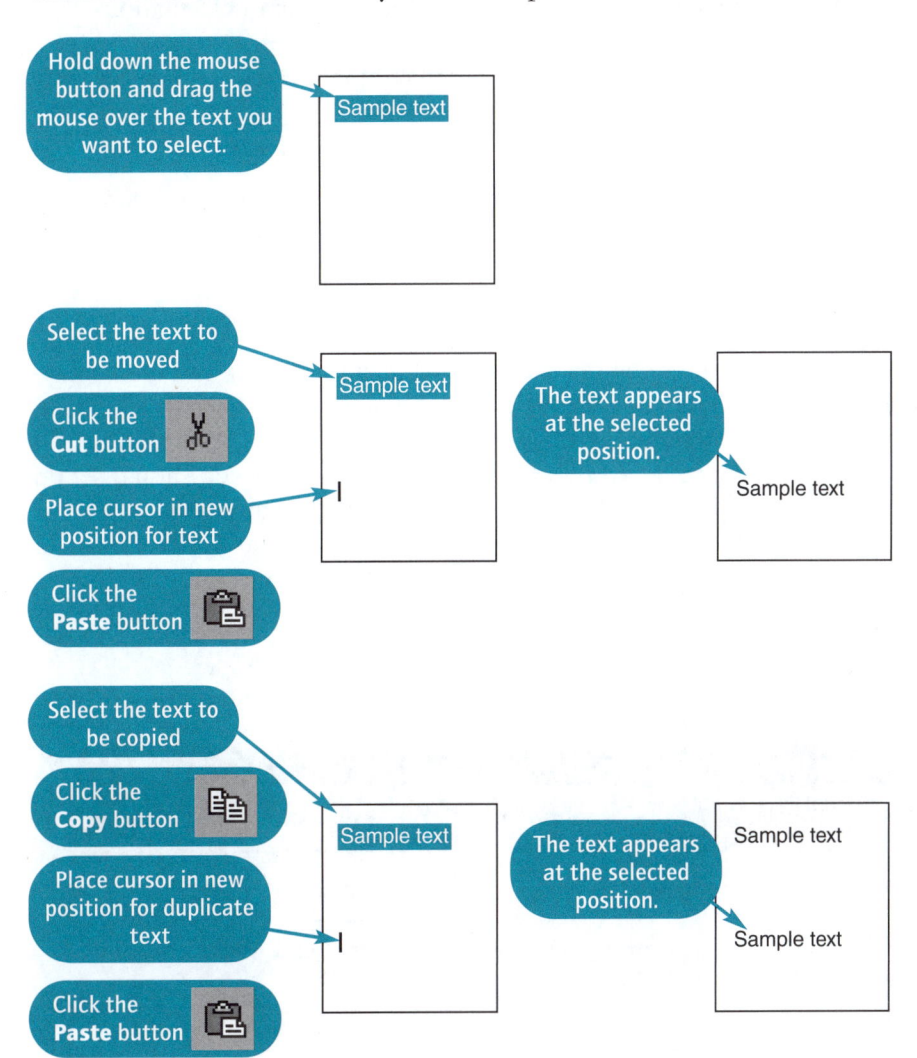

Editing text using Cut, Paste and Copy

Saving and finding work

You have spent hours at the computer, your work looks wonderful on-screen, but it will all be lost once you switch the computer off. So, when you have produced something on a computer, you need to save it somewhere on the computer. And when you have saved your work, you need to be able to find it again.

HARDWARE AND SOFTWARE | **7**

File organisation

Filing cabinets are boring but, when organised, we can quickly find data we have filed away. Computers may store your work on electronic disks but they are organised like filing cabinets. The files are divided up into folders:

- **File:** one document such as a letter, a report, a set of calculations.
- **File name:** your choice of name for a file.
- **Folder:** a collection of files on the same topic such as one subject you are studying, your emails or your hobbies.

Folders may also be called **directories** and they can be described as a tree with branches. A program like **Windows Explorer** can show this structure in a variety of ways.

Saving

Your computer may suggest you store your files in a folder called something like **My Documents** and this is a good start. When working on networks of computers, such as at college or school, the folders will already be in place for you. But on your own computer you should set up a personal system of folders with your own labels. Suppose you need to set up a new folder:

- Use **Windows Explorer** or a similar program
- Click on **File**, then **New** then **Folder**.
- Move down the directory of files and find the new folder.
- Click on the words 'New Folder' and type in your chosen name for it.

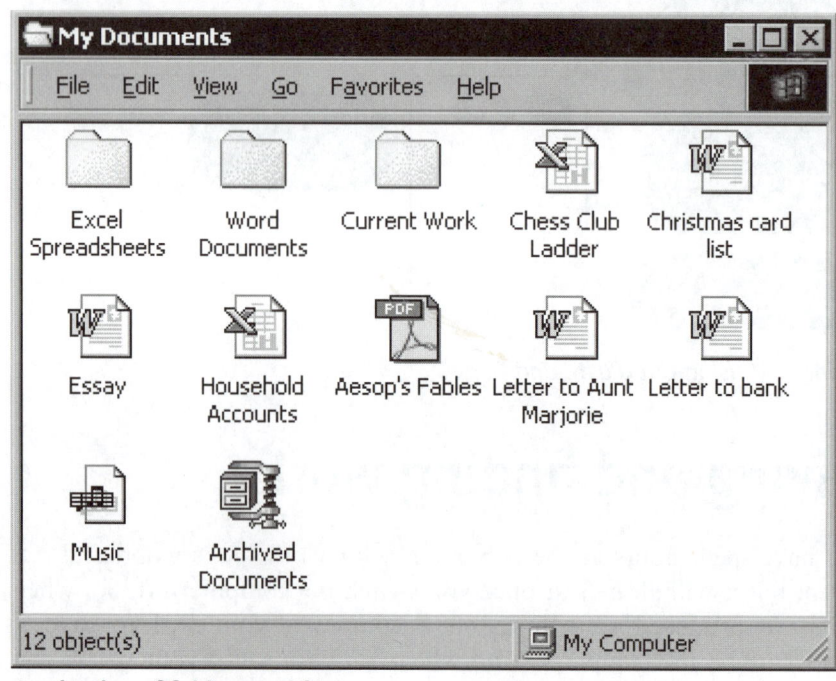

> **From IT helpdesk 'top ten'**
> I did save my work but I don't know where to find it!

A selection of folders and files

8 | THE LEARNING CURVE

> **LOST AND FOUND**
>
> Can't find a folder or file? Click on the Windows **Start** button, usually in the bottom left corner. Then click on the **Find** icon which pops up. Enter details in the boxes to start the finding process.

The first time you save your work, you will be asked for a file name. This is a label that you must think up and enter. At first you may be tempted by very short file names but, after losing your work and your memory a few times, you should use names which make reasonable sense. Earlier computer systems don't allow names longer than eight letters. Suppose you want to save a new document for the first time:

- At the top left of the screen click on **File**.
- Move down the menu and click on **Save as**.
- Click on the entry box labelled **Save in**.
- Select a folder to store the file in.
- Click on the entry box labelled **File name**.
- Type in your choice of name for the file.
- Click on the **Save** button.

After you have saved your work once, the computer interface usually remembers the last file name. Get into a routine of saving your work often and then you won't lose too much if you make a mistake or the power fails. Here are some occasions when you might save your work:

- Every five minutes
- Every new page
- When interrupted by someone
- When the phone rings
- When the cat approaches
- When you leave the computer, even for a moment

Programs, such as word processors, also have files which sit in their special folders with labels like **Windows**. Be careful not to save your personal files in these program folders. Also take care not to alter any program folders or files as it often stops the program working.

Old saying
Save often –
it costs nothing

Printing

Everything on the computer screen can be printed onto paper. We usually use a word processor or drawing package to produce paper copies. Before you print onto paper you can see exactly how it will look by using **Print preview**. The toolbar has an icon for this or you can pull down the **File** menu.

Options for printing

The program needs to match the page on your screen to the paper in your printer. Check this by clicking on **File** then **Page setup** and review the following options.

Checklist for printing
Printer connected to computer?
Printer switched on?
Paper loaded?
No paper jams?

HARDWARE AND SOFTWARE | 9

Options	Effect
Margins	Allows you to change the blank spaces between the edges of the paper and your work; the standard settings are usually good
Paper size	Allows you to change the size of paper; A4 paper is the usual choice.
Orientation	Allows you to print across the paper; normal printing is down the paper (portrait) but for some projects you might print across the paper (landscape)

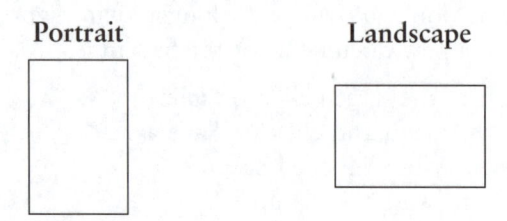

Portrait   Landscape

When you are ready to print, choose which pages and how many copies.

Options	Effect
Number of copies	The standard setting is to print one copy, but it can be any number
All pages	Will print all pages of your document, including any blanks at the end
Current page	Will print just the page which is on-screen when you start the **Print** command
Some pages	Will print just the pages that you put in the box or boxes, e.g. 3-6 will print pages 3, 4, 5 and 6

Advanced features of programs

Templates

A template is a ready-made document or system which supplies you with layout, font sizes and styles, and other effects to make your document look good in print. The document may be blank or it may contain dummy headings and text for you to change to your own.

The popular word processors, spreadsheets and databases usually supply templates which are available when you give the command **File New**. You may be offered a choice of different categories such as letters, faxes or publications. You then need to choose a certain style such as contemporary or traditional. Above all, you need to check that the style is suitable for your purpose; see the section on presenting information. Here are some typical steps in making a new template:

- Start a new document.
- Choose and set:
    - font
    - margins
    - paper size
    - other effects
- Type some sample text if you like.
- Select **Save as**.
- Pull down the **Save as type** menu and select **template**.
- Give the template a name and **Save**.

To use the template:

- Use the **File New** command.
- Select your template by its name.
- Type over the top of the template.
- Use the **Save as** command and give a new name.

Macros

If you often need to repeat a task in a program, entering your own address in a document for example, then you can automate the task using a **macro**. A macro is a series of commands grouped together in a single command. Instead of repeating a series of actions, you can issue the single command that carries out that task. Some typical uses for macros:

- Faster and easier routine editing
- Faster and easier routine formatting
- Executing multiple commands
- Automating a complex set of tasks

The full versions of programs like word processors databases, and spreadsheets allow you to create macros by turning on a recorder which tracks your sequence of commands and instructions. When finished, you can save this sequence under a label with its own special keystroke or icon. You can also create and modify macros using a programming language such as **Visual Basic**.

Databases

A database is usually a large set of information, such as the records of an organisation. The information is held in computer records and files. The term 'database' may also be used for the computer program which handles the files.

Information retrieval is about obtaining information you have specified from a large store of information.

Uses of databases

A database is used whenever you need to do the following types of task:

- Holding lots of information, e.g. the details of everyone who has car insurance with a company
- Sorting files into a different order, e.g. listing in order of name or type of car
- Searching all information and producing lists, e.g. listing all people who need to renew insurance this month
- Getting statistics, e.g. counting how many cars are of a certain make or calculating the average value

You don't have to have a huge amount of information to use a database. A good example of a simple database is a collection of names and addresses for people and you might already keep them in address books or on card files. The computer versions of simple databases often have names like Address Book or Cardfile.

Database programs
Access
Approach
FileMaker
Paradox

Database structure

A computer database of information needs to be organised with a structure. It is useful to think of a collection of information on cards when dealing with the items of a database:

- **A field** contains one item of information about a person, such as the name, town or phone number.
- **A record** contains all the information for one person, such as on one card in the file.
- **The database** is the full collection of records.

When you buy a ready-made database, like the address list in an email

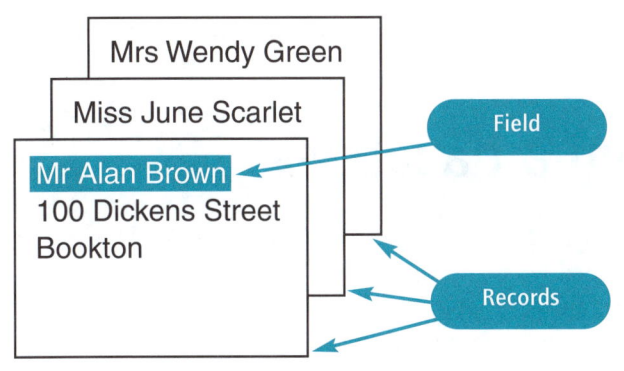

Parts of a database

program, it will already have a structure. You just need to enter the information, with one record for each person. In other databases you will be asked to invent the fields and tell the program the type of data to expect in each field. Here are some data types:

- **Text:** letters of the alphabet such as names, and some numbers used for labels such as phone numbers.
- **Number:** numbers used for calculation, such as finding the average age.
- **Date:** numbers meaning dates such as 23/10/01.
- **Logical:** these usually have the value TRUE or FALSE.

Look at the diagram that shows the database records of 10 people, together with their towns and their ages. This information is laid out in the form of a grid or table. It is the raw information before any sorting of filtering.

Month, day, year is the US convention for giving dates.

Forename	Surname	Town	Age
James	Goodman	Northtown	16
Elizabeth	Baker	Northtown	18
Michael	King	Southport	15
Neville	Madden	Southport	19
Kirit	Patel	Northtown	16
Michael	Schofield	Westville	21
Mary	King	Northtown	16
Paulo	Dias	Westville	16
Nita	Bhudia	Southport	17
Peter	Zhang	Northtown	20

Sample database

The complete information about a single person makes up one **record** of data. The records can be entered in any order, providing that you put each item of information in its correct **field**. In this database the fields are

USING DATABASES | 13

forename, surname, town and age. The power of the database will allow us to sort it then search it.

Output from a database

To use a database we normally ask for some output or result. This result might be a particular record we want, or it might be a sorted list of names. Most databases have ready-made commands which let you sort and find simple information. Here are some typical outputs we might get from the example database.

All data, sorted in order of surname

Forename	Surname	Town	Age
Elizabeth	Baker	Northtown	18
Nita	Bhudia	Southport	17
Paulo	Dias	Westville	16
James	Goodman	Northtown	16
Michael	King	Southport	15
Mary	King	Northtown	16
Neville	Madden	Southport	19
Kirit	Patel	Northtown	16
Michael	Schofield	Westville	21
Peter	Zhang	Northtown	20

All data, sorted in order of age

Forename	Surname	Town	Age
Michael	King	Southport	15
Paulo	Dias	Westville	16
James	Goodman	Northtown	16
Mary	King	Northtown	16
Kirit	Patel	Northtown	16
Nita	Bhudia	Southport	17
Elizabeth	Baker	Northtown	18
Neville	Madden	Southport	19
Peter	Zhang	Northtown	20
Michael	Schofield	Westville	21

Data filtered to match the town of Southport

Forename	Surname	Town	Age
Michael	King	Southport	15
Nita	Bhudia	Southport	17
Neville	Madden	Southport	

Selection of different outputs from the sample database

Searching a database

See also: **Searching the Internet**, page 19.

To use a database you need to be able to look through all the records and find what you want:

- **A query** is a search of a database with a set of conditions.
- **A match** is when the computer finds a record which agrees with your conditions.
- **A report** is a list of all the records which obey the conditions.

Suppose you want to find all records in a database that have the surname Goodman. This is your query or search condition. Different databases can ask you to enter your condition in different ways. Some examples are shown in the following table.

Query methods	Action	Note
Entry box with label such as **Find What?**	Enter **Goodman** in box	Simple databases of addresses use this method
A query table which allows you to copy an example on-screen	Enter **Goodman** in table under surname label	Popular databases use this method
Entry line for you to enter a mathematical condition	Enter **Town= Southport**	Lists all records where the town is Southport
	Enter **Age>16**	Lists all records where the age is greater than 16

Advanced queries

Searches can involve multiple combinations of queries using keywords like AND, OR; and the logic of expressions using keywords TRUE, FALSE. The following table shows examples which relate to the sample database on page 14.

Search shorthand
a = b   a equals b
a > b   a is greater than b
a < b   a is less than b
a<>b   a not equal to b

Query	Meaning	Outputs records for
surname=King AND town=Northport	Lists only those records where the surname is King and also the town is Northport	Mary King
surname=King NOT town=Northport	Lists only those records where the surname is King and also the town is not Northport	Michael King*
town=Southport AND Age>16	Lists only those records where the town is Southport and also the age is greater than 16	Bhudia Madden
town=Southport OR town=Westville	Lists any records where the town is Southport or the town is Westville	Bhudia Dias King Madden Schofield

* Sometimes there may not be a record.

USING DATABASES | 15

Using the Internet

When computers are connected together they make a network, such as you might get in a school or college. On a larger scale you can have a wide area network (WAN), such as when cash dispensers in the streets are linked to large computers in the banks. The main types of network are:

- Local area network (LAN)
- Wide area network (WAN)
- World Wide Web (WWW)

The Internet is a system which allows many computers in the world to join together a system of link-ups. The Internet is effectively a huge database of information and the rules for retrieving data are similar to those used to query databases. At home we usually link to the Internet via our phone line but larger computers in the Internet are connected by high-speed telecommunication links which use cable and satellite.

The Web

The Internet can be used in different ways but the two main uses for most people are **email**, described in a later section, and the **Web**. The Web is part of the Internet where organisations or people have pages of text and pictures. From these pages you can find information, buy goods or jump to other pages. You get directly to a **website** by entering the address into your browser. Website addresses often look like this:

www.name.com

www.name.co.uk

Looking up websites

To use the Internet you subscribe to an **internet service provider** (ISP) who has a computer which links you to the Web. Your local computer is connected to your ISP by using a modem which sends digital signals along the phone connections. Your computer will have an icon for dial-up connections. Click on this icon to connect to the Internet; you may need to enter a password before the modem begins to dial. The computers at work, in

---

Internet activities

send and receive email
check football scores
update news
browse catalogues
book holidays
shop and buy
buy and sell at auctions
check TV and films
book cinema tickets
visit museums
play/download music
play games
visit fan clubs
read books
chat with friends
check your bank

an Internet cafe, or in a college are usually permanently connected to the Internet.

When you're online to the Web you will use a **browser,** such as **Microsoft Explorer** or **Netscape Navigator**. The browser is a computer program which displays webpages.

Using a browser

All types of browser work in a similar manner and have a banner along the top of the screen where you click to give commands. The main commands are described in the following table.

Icon	Effect when clicked
Address or Go to	Allows you to enter the address or name of a website that you want
Back	Takes you back to the webpage you just visited
Forward	Moves you forward to a webpage you just came from
Stop	Stops loading the current page
Refresh or Reload	Loads a new version of the current page; useful when a page is incomplete or often updated
Home	Goes to the page seen when your browser opens; this can be changed to whatever you want
Search	Begins options which search by keyword
Favourites or Bookmarks	Drops down a list of favourite websites you have marked in the past
Mail	Connects to email
History	Gives a list of the websites you have visited in past days or weeks
Mail	Opens the options for using email
Print	Prints out the webpage shown on-screen

STOP BUTTON

Click the **Stop** button if a connection is very slow; you can try again at a less busy time.

The most important thing is to get started using the blank line near the top of the screen called **Address** or **Go to**. Suppose you want to see the website with address www.bbc.co.uk:

- Type it into the address box of your browser.
- Check you have typed it correctly.
- Press the **Enter** key.
- Wait for the webpage to download into your computer.

Some ISPs
AOL
BT Internet
Bun
Claranet
Compuserve
Freeserve
Virgin Net

Web addresses
Most website addresses start with **www**.

USING THE INTERNET | **17**

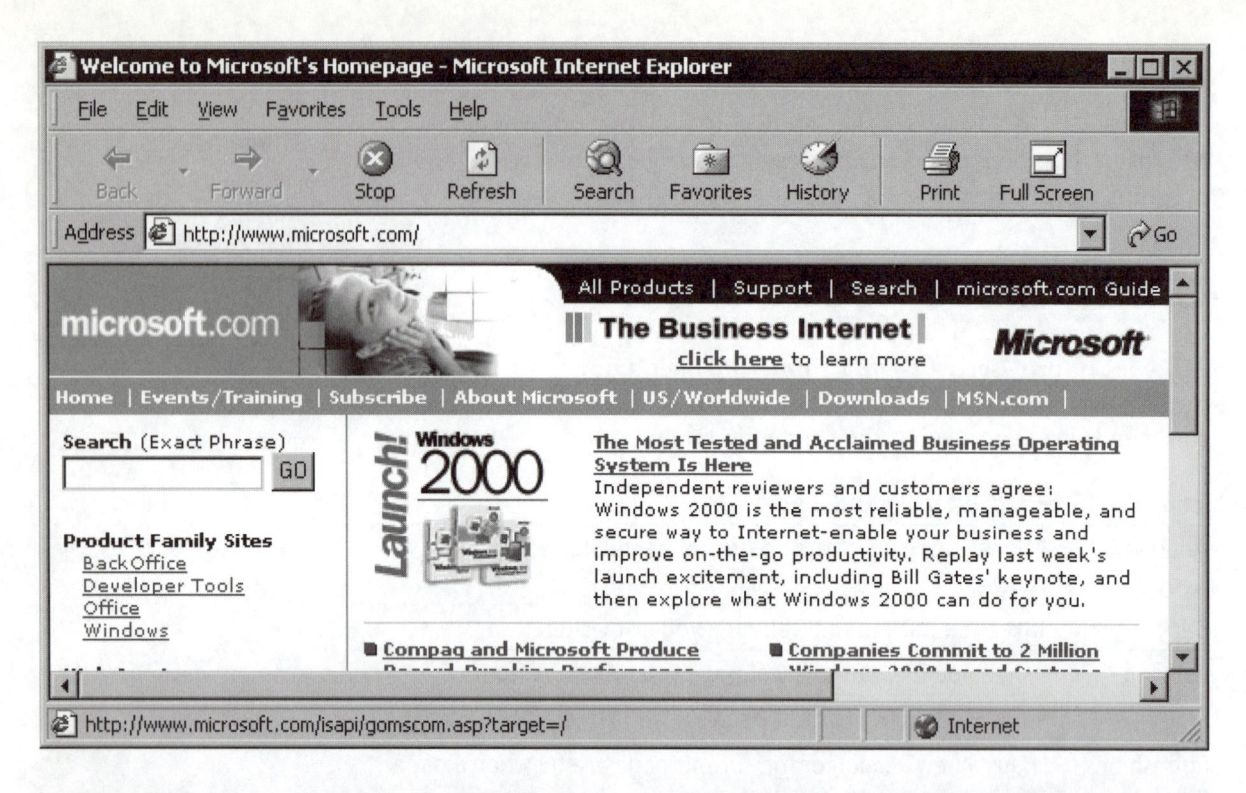

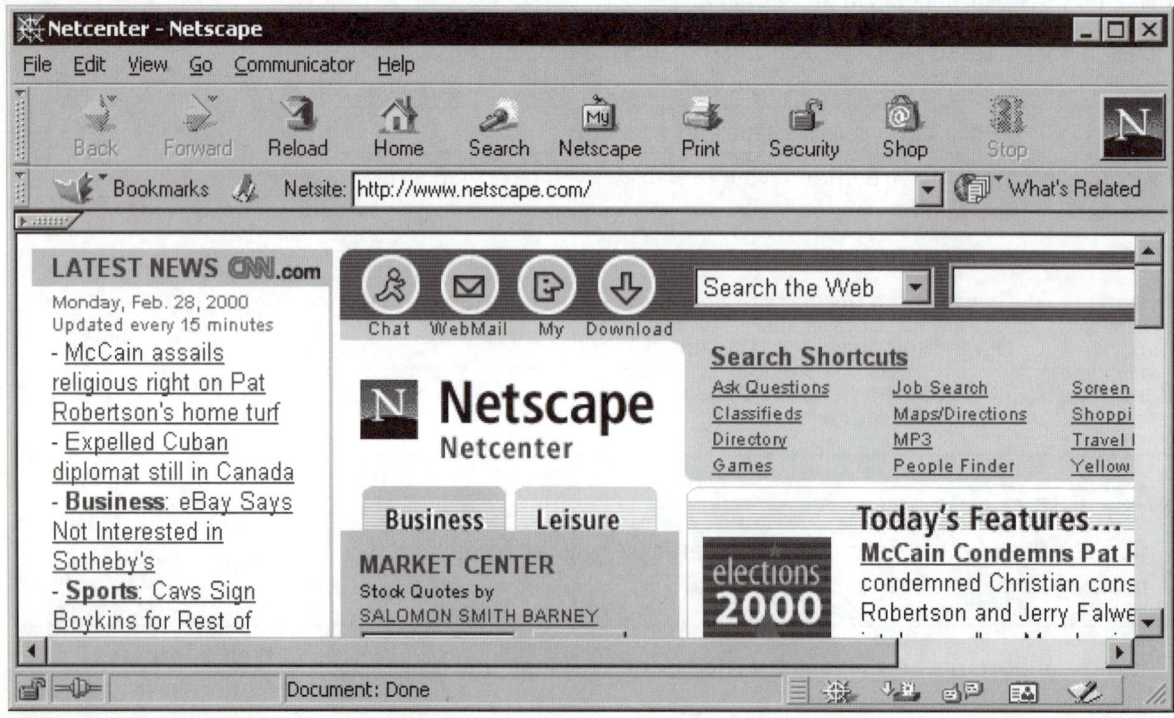

Internet browsers: Internet Explorer and Netscape

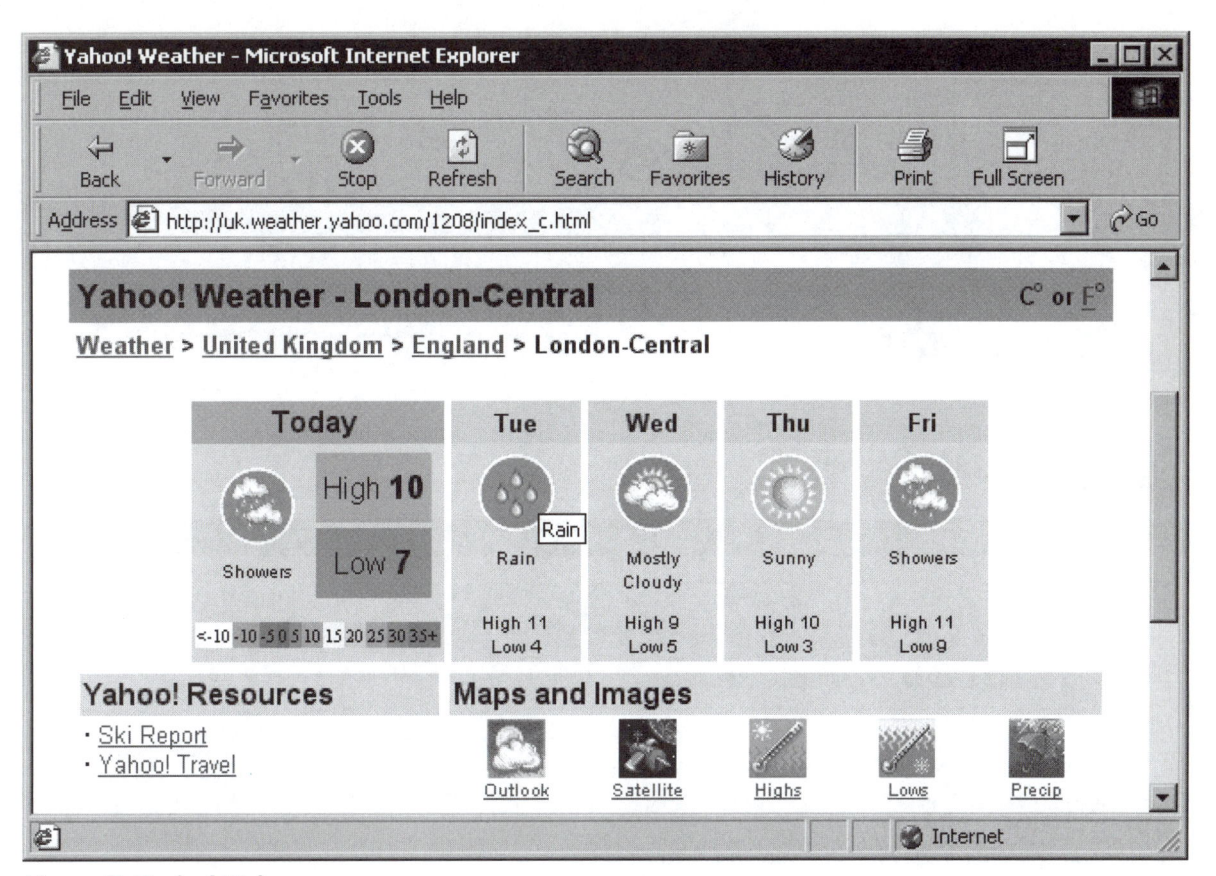

Figure 11 Typical Web page

Searching the Internet

The Internet joins you to the information held by thousands of computers world wide, so it is the largest database in the world. Somewhere on the Internet are websites with answers to your questions, but they have to be found. You can reach this information in the following two ways:

- **Go directly** because you know the website address.
- **Use a search engine** to trawl the net for relevant websites.

Search engines

Some well-known search engines are described in the following table. Some of the engines let you enter your question in general language. Others work better if you use the tricks for advanced searches.

Popular search engines
AltaVista
AskJeeves
Excite
Google
HotBot
Infoseek
Lycos
MSN Search
Northern Light
Yahoo

See also: **Searching a database**, page 12.

USING THE INTERNET | **19**

Two typical search engines (AskJeeves and AltaVista)

Search engine and address	Notes
AskJeeves **www.ask.co.uk**	Good site for beginners. Allows you to ask questions in plain English such as, Where is information about xyz? Some of the answers may be too general
MSN Search **www.search.msn.com**	Good site for beginners and good links to other information
Yahoo **www.yahoo.co.uk**	Can be browsed by categories or can be searched by keyword
AltaVista **www.altavista.com**	Indexes more webpages than many engines. Also has advanced search option to focus your search

Advanced searches

Some types of search involve the logic of combinations. This is particularly true when searching huge databases like the Internet. For example, searching for 'spice girls' could bring you thousands of references for 'spice' as in cooking and 'girls' as in girls.

But if you want to find the pop group Spice Girls then you can link the two words together by using AND. This will force the search engine to look for references where the words are joined together. Here is how you search for websites on blue whales.

Extra search conditions (word or symbol)	*Possible effect*
AND +	Will find references which include the word *blue* joined with the word *whales*. This condition will probably find the references to the particular type of whale
OR –	Will find references which include either the word *blue* or the word *whales*. This condition will find thousands of references you don't want

Search shorthand
a = b   first equals the second
a > b   a is greater than b
a < b   a is less than be

USING THE INTERNET | **21**

Spreadsheets

Spreadsheets are programs which allow you to enter numerical data and then see what happens when you change some values. They are good places to store numerical information because they can sort the numbers and turn them into graphs if you like.

Spreadsheets look like a big sheet of paper with a grid of boxes or a table. The clever thing is that each box, or cell, contains its own calculator and word processor, and these cells can be linked together to do useful things. Changing just one number on-screen causes all other numbers to be updated automatically.

A spreadsheet is included in most collections of computer software; here are some possible uses:

- Calculator
- Quick graphs
- Estimates of cost
- Invoices
- Profit and loss
- Business plans
- Models and graphs
- Mathematics

Graphs
All spreadsheets can turn your numbers into smart graphs.

Some spreadsheets
Excel
1-2-3
Ability
Works

Using a spreadsheet

All spreadsheet programs work in the same general way and have the same basic layout. In any cell you can enter the following types of information:

- **Text:** usually labels such as Sales or January.
- **Numbers:** usually data such as sales figures.
- **Formulas:** A1+A2 will add the contents of cell A1 and cell A2.

Above the basic worksheet of cells on-screen there are standard menus and icons where you can give commands to the spreadsheet. For example, there may be icons which make it easy to add numbers, sort columns of data and produce graphs.

When you change any number on-screen the formulas will automatically recalculate all other numbers and show the new results. That's the point of a spreadsheet.

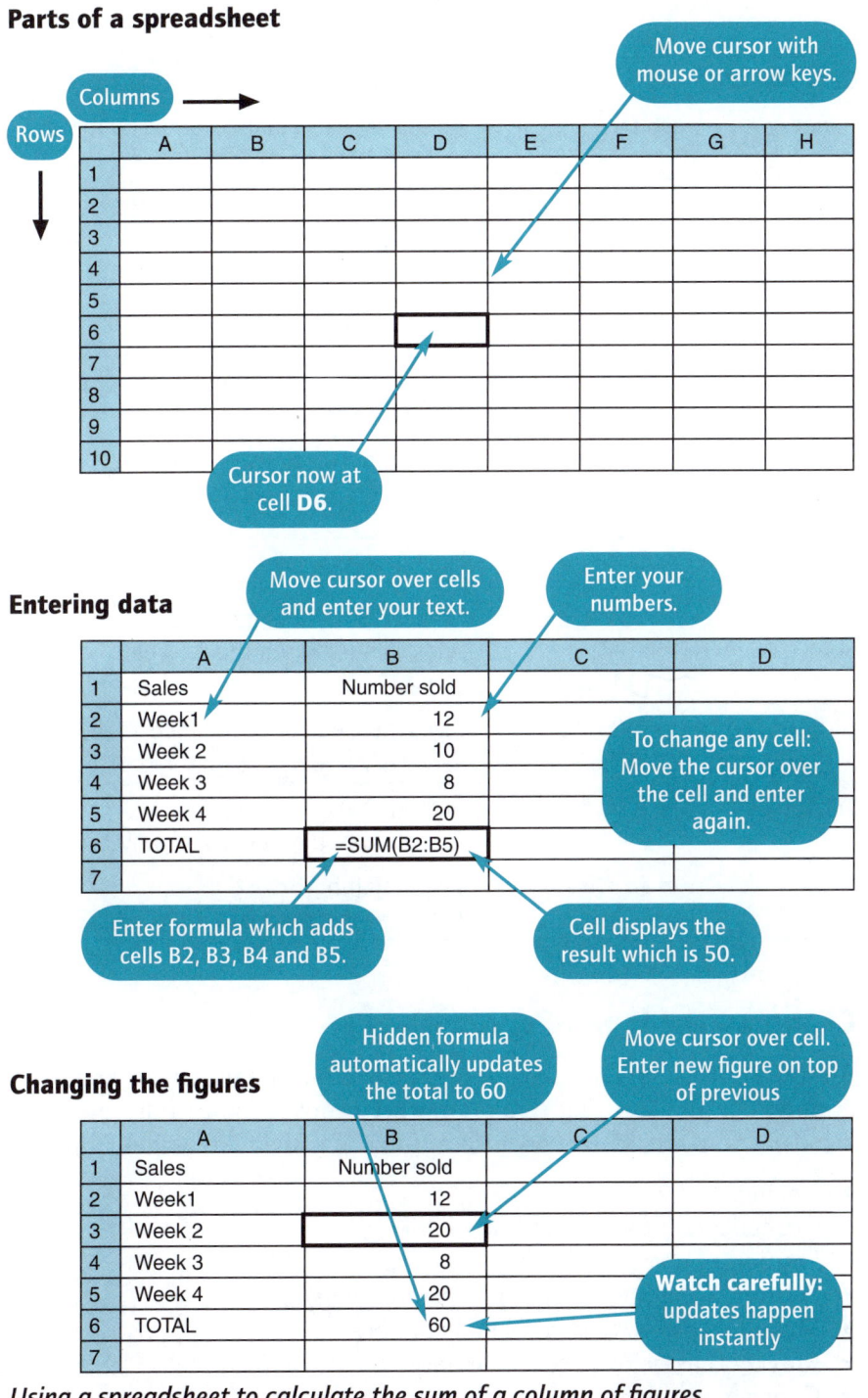

Parts of a spreadsheet

Columns →

Rows ↓

	A	B	C	D	E	F	G	H
1								
2								
3								
4								
5								
6								
7								
8								
9								
10								

Move cursor with mouse or arrow keys.

Cursor now at cell **D6**.

Entering data

Move cursor over cells and enter your text.

Enter your numbers.

	A	B	C	D
1	Sales	Number sold		
2	Week1	12		
3	Week 2	10		
4	Week 3	8		
5	Week 4	20		
6	TOTAL	=SUM(B2:B5)		
7				

To change any cell: Move the cursor over the cell and enter again.

Enter formula which adds cells B2, B3, B4 and B5.

Cell displays the result which is 50.

Changing the figures

Hidden formula automatically updates the total to 60

Move cursor over cell. Enter new figure on top of previous

	A	B	C	D
1	Sales	Number sold		
2	Week1	12		
3	Week 2	20		
4	Week 3	8		
5	Week 4	20		
6	TOTAL	60		
7				

Watch carefully: updates happen instantly

Using a spreadsheet to calculate the sum of a column of figures

SPREADSHEETS | 23

Spreadsheet formulas

A spreadsheet has more mathematical power than most people can ever use. But you should at least learn the useful features such as automatically adding a set of numbers or producing an average. Here are some common symbols used for spreadsheet maths.

Entry	Typical example	Effect
Cell reference	D6	Refers to the cell in column D at row 6
Range	D6:D10	All the cells in column D between row 6 and row 10
=		Enter = to start all maths in spreadsheets
+	= 3+3 = A1+A2	Addition
–	= 8–3 = A1–A2	Subtraction
*	= 8*3 = 8*D6	Multiplication
/	= 8/3 = D6/A1	Division
%	= 100+17.5%	Percentage
^	= 10^3	Exponent or power, e.g. $10^3 = 1000$
SUM	= SUM (A1:A22)	Adds all numbers in the cells between A1 and A22
AVERAGE	= AVERAGE (A1:A22)	Gives the mean of all numbers in the cells between A1 and A22
>	= A1>B1	Greater than Tells you whether it is TRUE or FALSE
<	= A1<B1	Less than (nl) Tells you whether it is TRUE or FALSE

Changing the look of spreadsheets

All spreadsheets can have their appearance changed; this may be useful for printing out and showing results to other people. You can use the commands of your particular spreadsheet to change the following features:

- Column widths
- Changing text to bold and other effects
- Position of text in cell (left, centre, right)
- Position of number in cell (left, centre, right)
- Making gaps between rows and columns
- Moving cells or rows and columns
- Copying cells or rows and columns

Charts and graphs

All spreadsheets allow you to convert a set of figures into a graph or a choice of graphs. It is worth entering a set of your figures into a spreadsheet just to get a good graph. Here are some of the possibilities.

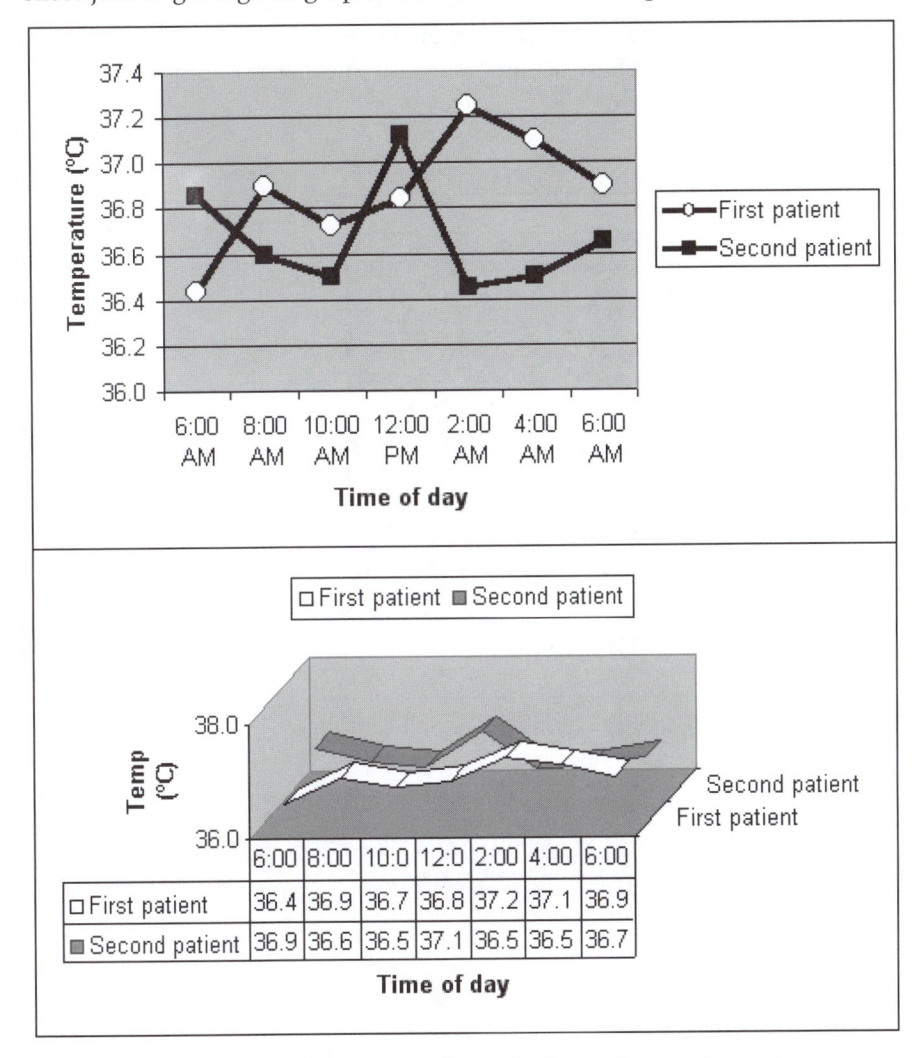

Two graphs created within a spreadsheet (both graphs use the same information)

Suppose you want to convert some numerical data into a chart or graph, perhaps the link between people's weight and height.

Entering the data
- Start a new spreadsheet which is blank.
- Enter the names for labels into separate cells, e.g. Weight, Height.
- Enter the values for (weight, height) pairs into separate cells.

Weight (kg)	61	63	64	65	66	66	67	67
Height (cm)	152	157	165	165	170	175	177	182

SPREADSHEETS | 25

Making the graph
- Select the labels and the numbers that you want to see as a graph.
- Use the **Tools** menu or the chart icon to start the chart making.
- Use the options to choose the type of graph.
- Use the options to point to the labels and to add headings.
- Use the **View** menu to preview the effect.
- You can print the chart or import it into another program such as your word processor.

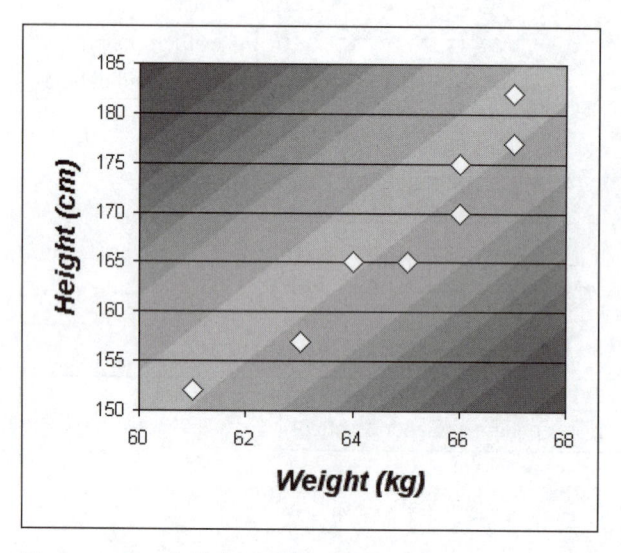

Your graph might look like this!

Word processors

Word processors (WPs) let you compose your words on the screen and then edit the words or the layout before you print onto paper. So you really are processing words. You can change the size and style of the printing on the page and add items such as graphs, photos or other images. Most word processors also allow you to produce enhanced layouts such as columns, bullets or tables. They can also automatically send a similar letter to many people with personalised details, such as names and addresses.

Word processors
Word
SmartSuite
WordPerfect
Works
Ability Office
WordPad

Word processor features

All word processors work in the same general way and have the following basic features:

- **Writing text** allows you to enter your work at the keyboard.
- **File commands** allow work to be saved, opened, previewed and printed.
- **Edit commands** allow work to be changed using undo, cut, paste and copy.
- **View commands** allow changes to the look of the word processor on-screen.
- **Insert commands** allow pictures and other effects to be brought in from other programs or files.
- **Format commands** allow changes to the type style and parge layout.

WYSIWYG

The normal operation of a word processor is WYSIYWYG (what you see is what you get), which means that the styles and layout you see on-screen will be the same on the printout.

CHAPTER TITLE | 27

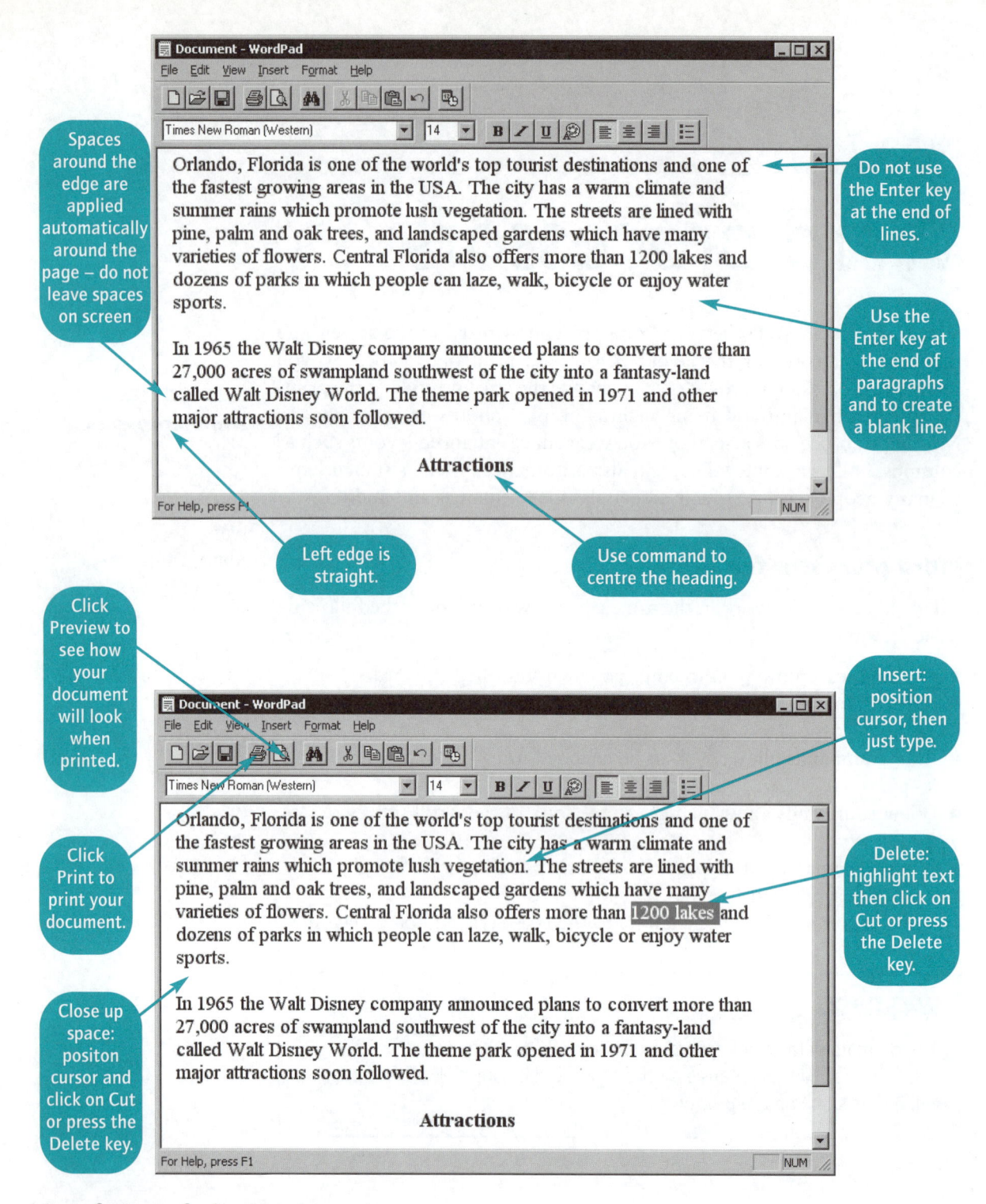

WordPad document (first screenshot) annotations:

- Spaces around the edge are applied automatically around the page – do not leave spaces on screen
- Do not use the Enter key at the end of lines.
- Use the Enter key at the end of paragraphs and to create a blank line.
- Left edge is straight.
- Use command to centre the heading.

Document text shown in WordPad:

Orlando, Florida is one of the world's top tourist destinations and one of the fastest growing areas in the USA. The city has a warm climate and summer rains which promote lush vegetation. The streets are lined with pine, palm and oak trees, and landscaped gardens which have many varieties of flowers. Central Florida also offers more than 1200 lakes and dozens of parks in which people can laze, walk, bicycle or enjoy water sports.

In 1965 the Walt Disney company announced plans to convert more than 27,000 acres of swampland southwest of the city into a fantasy-land called Walt Disney World. The theme park opened in 1971 and other major attractions soon followed.

Attractions

Second screenshot annotations:

- Click Preview to see how your document will look when printed.
- Click Print to print your document.
- Close up space: positon cursor and click on Cut or press the Delete key.
- Insert: position cursor, then just type.
- Delete: highlight text then click on Cut or press the Delete key.

Some features of using a word processor

28 | THE LEARNING CURVE

Changing formats

The letters and other characters you see on-screen and on paper can be shown in different sizes and designs. A **typeface** or **font** is a set of characters of a particular design. Here are some examples:

- This font is regular
- *This font is italic*
- **This font is bold**
- ***This font is bold italic***

Font size

The sizes of characters are measured by an old system called **points**. Books and journas use type sizes between 10 and 12 points; 72 point type means there is about one inch from a character's baseline to the baseline above.

Font design

The letters that you see on-screen or on paper have a particular look, and each look has a name, e.g. Times Roman or Univers. The different designs can be put into two main families depending upon whether the letters are plain or whether they have little projections called serifs:

- **With serifs:** characters with wide ends, like the words in the paragraph above.
- **Without serifs:** plain characters, like the words in the table on the next page.

Font with serifs

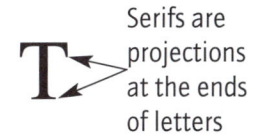

T — Serifs are projections at the ends of letters

You can experiment with different looks in different sizes. Professional designers often use two different fonts. If you use too many different fonts, your text will look very busy.

SPECIAL SYMBOLS

There are lots of symbols you can put in your documents. In most programs, click on the **Insert** menu, click on **Symbol** and then choose **Symbols** or **Wingdings** or similar. Here are some examples:

✂ ✉ ✈ ✂ ☺ ✗ ✓ ✳ ✆ → ❖ ☞ © 🍎 ⓘ 🍽 🅿

Layout of documents

When text is presented for other people to read, its layout needs to have breaks and variety, otherwise it is uninviting to look at and boring to read. Here are a summary and a few examples.

CHAPTER TITLE | **29**

Layout method	Notes	How to do it *
Margins	Plenty of white paper around the edge of the text usually looks good	Use **File** then **Page setup** and **Margins**
Paragraphs	Paragraphs are groups of sentences separated by a blank line or an indent	Press the **Enter** key at the end of a paragraph
Blank lines	The word processor includes enough space between lines for comfortable reading. But you can add extra lines for special effects	Press the **Enter** key for a new line, twice for a blank line
New page	New subjects or chapters usually start on a new page	Click on **Insert** then **Break**
Text aligned left	Starts each line against the left margin. This is a normal printing layout	Click on **Format** then **Paragraph**
Text aligned left and right (justified)	Starts each line against the left margin and also lines up the right edge of the text. This gives an effect like a newspaper column	Click on **Format** then **Paragraph****
Text centred	Text is arranged in the middle of the page	Click on **Format** then **Paragraph****
Tabs	Tabs are set positions on a line that the cursor jumps to. Useful for lining up columns of figures	Click on **Format** then **Tabs**
Bullet lists	Bullet points are blobs at the beginning of a line. They are useful in lists and to give variety	Click on **Format** then **Bullets and Numbering**
Numbered lists	Numbered lists are like bullet lists but their items have numbers instead of bullets. The numbers usually count up from 1	Use **Format** then **Bullets and Numbering**
Tables	Full office-based word processors create grids of spaces into which you can place your text	Use the **Table** menu

* This is how to do it with a mouse but there may be keyboard shortcuts, icons and other menus.
** Spaces are added automatically.

Left aligned

Orlando, Florida is one of the world's top tourist destinations and one of the fastest growing areas in the USA. The city has a warm climate and summer rains which promote lush pine, palm and oak trees, and landscaped gardens which have many varieties of flowers.

Right edge is jagged.

Left edge is straight.

Justified

Orlando, Florida is one of the world's top tourist destinations and one of the fastest growing areas in the USA. The city has a warm climate and summer rains which promote lush pine, palm and oak trees, and landscaped gardens which have many varieties of flowers.

Right edge is straight. This makes extra gaps in the text.

Left edge is straight.

Centred

Orlando attractions include:
Epcot
Gatorland
King Henry's Feast
Pirate's Dinner Adventure
Ripley's Believe It or Not
Seaworld
Terror on Church Street
Universal Studios
Walt Disney World
Wet 'n' Wild

Each line is in the centre of the page.

Bulleted

Orlando attractions include:
- Epcot
- Gatorland
- King Henry's Feast
- Pirate's Dinner Adventure
- Ripley's Believe It or Not
- Seaworld
- Terror on Church Street
- Universal Studios
- Walt Disney World
- Wet 'n' Wild

Each line has a big dot (bullet) in front.

Different document layouts

Advanced word processor features

Most office word processors have these features:

- **Headers and footers** show a label across the top and bottom of each page; they can include the page number.
- **Tables present** a grid on the page into which you can insert numbers and words; you can show or hide their borders.
- **Templates are** stored styles and formats contained in empty documents; they can be used to start new documents, e.g. a standard letter.
- **Mail merge** allows you to print many personalised letters from a single form letter; the information is taken from a data file containing names, addresses and other data.
- **Macros are** pre-recorded routines or programs which automatically carry out common tasks such as writing the date.
- **Security passwords** protect files from being read or changed.
- **Word count** totals the words and other features in a document.
- **Mathematics** can be applied to any columns or rows of figures in the document.

Checking and proof-reading

Computer programs are powerful but they aren't perfect at all tasks. For example, the spellchecker on your word processor is useful but can only alert you if the word is not in the dictionary. A spellchecker will not notice if you have used the wrong word for the job. Here are some other ways of checking your work:

- Ask other people to look at your work
- Wait a while before you check your work
- Print the work and check it on paper

Graphics

Graphics are any pictures or graphs produced by your computer. Most computers have at least one graphics packages; Windows has Paint.

Paint packages

A **paint package** is a computer program which lets you do freehand drawing and colouring on-screen. You can also take other images, such as scanned photos and drawings, and adapt them for your own purposes.

There is a paint program, often called Paint or Paintbrush, included in most collections of computer software; you can use it to achieve the following effects:

- Making simple drawings
- Graphics for reports
- Making changes to photos
- Viewing imported images
- Making computer wallpaper

All paint programs work in the same general way and have the following basic features:

- **Lines and curves** can be set at different thicknesses.
- **Standard shapes** are circles, ovals, squares and rectangles.
- **Pen or brush** can be set to produce lines, blobs, stipples and other textures.
- **Colours** are selected from a palette and poured into shapes.
- **Patterns** can be used instead of colours or with colours.
- **Rubber** lets you rub out mistakes or change your mind.
- **Edit commands** allow work to be changed using undo, cut, paste and copy.
- **Shaping commands** allow you to trim, stretch and rotate.
- **View commands** allow different magnifications.
- **Insert commands** allow pictures and other effects to be brought in from other programs or files.

Paint programs work by changing the **pixels** (dots) on your computer display. When you try to enlarge an image from a paint program, you will begin to notice the square areas of the pixels. If this is a problem then you need to consider using another type of program, such as CAD.

Some graphics
symbols such as ✔
freehand drawings
clip art
scanned photos
charts and graphs
computer-aided design
3D models
animation

See also:
Spreadsheets,
page 22.

Paint features
generate lines and shapes
fill with colour
add text
give brush effects
cut, copy and paste
zoom in or out
rotate and stretch
insert pictures

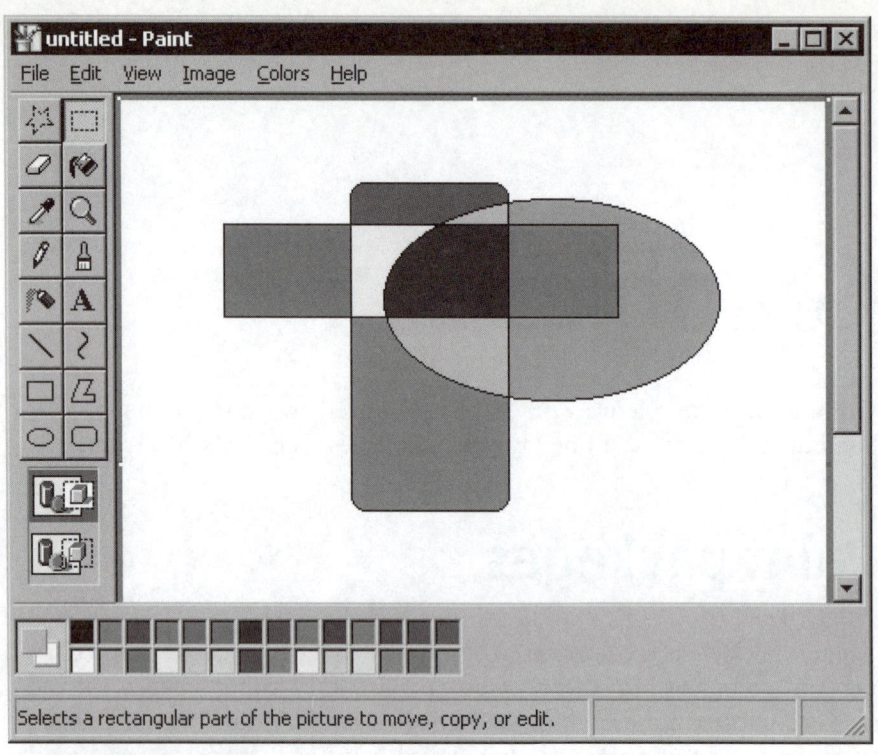

Typical painting program

Computer-aided design

Pixels: the smallest area, or dot, that makes the image.

Vectors: sets of coordinates which describe the image.

Computer-aided design (CAD) software allows you to produce very precise drawings, to perhaps 16 decimal places of accuracy. CAD achieves this accuracy by storing **vectors** or **objects** (e.g. lines) in the form of mathematical information. It does not depend upon the number of pixels on your screen.

The accuracy and the other features of CAD have many applications:

- Architectural drawings
- Engineering drawings
- Maps
- Geographic information systems (GIS)

Typical features of a CAD package include:

- A set of grid lines
- Coordinates and accurate measurements
- Standard libraries of shapes and components
- Accurate changes to drawings by scaling, rotation and movement
- Calculations based on the drawing, e.g. dimensions and areas
- Automatic conversion into new views, e.g. 3D projections
- Interface to specialised input devices, e.g. tablets
- Interface to specialised output devices, e.g. plotters or machinery

34 | THE LEARNING CURVE

Communicating

Using email

Electronic mail, or email, is a system on the Internet which allows you to send messages and other computer files to any other user who has a computer connected to the Internet. When your computer is not connected to the Internet, the incoming messages are stored by your internet service provider (ISP).

The ISP has a computer which links you to the Web. You connect your computer to your ISP using a modem and a special phone number. Your computer will have an icon for dial-up connections. Click on this icon to dial into your ISP and check your email. You may need to enter a password. At work, college or school your computers may be permanently connected to the Internet.

An email program is computer software which lets you exchange messages with other users connected to the Internet. You can normally use it for these functions:

- Prepare and store messages before sending
- Send messages to other users
- Send messages to groups of users
- Receive messages from other users
- Scan and read the messages received
- Send a reply to any message
- Print out messages onto paper
- Send and receive computer files with messages
- Delete or store messages
- Store favourite email addresses

Email can be used to send and receive text, pictures, videos and sound. With some software packages it is even possible to make phone calls to another user who has similar equipment. All email programs work in the same general way and have the following basic features:

- **Header** is where you enter the email address of the person to get the message, anyone who is to get a copy, the subject of the message.
- **The body** is where you type the text of the message. You can cut and paste text from elsewhere, such as a word processor.

Online means connected to the Internet.
Offline means not connected to the Internet.

Email programs
Eudora
Outlook
cc:Mail
Hotmail/Webmail

- **Address book** is where you can store the email addresses of people you know.
- **Signature** automatically adds your chosen signature and other details at the end of the message.
- **Reply options** let you return a message to the sender without typing in the email address.
- **Reply to all** lets you return your message to the sender plus anyone who was on the copy list.
- **Forward** lets you pass the email on to someone new, perhaps adding a comment of your own.

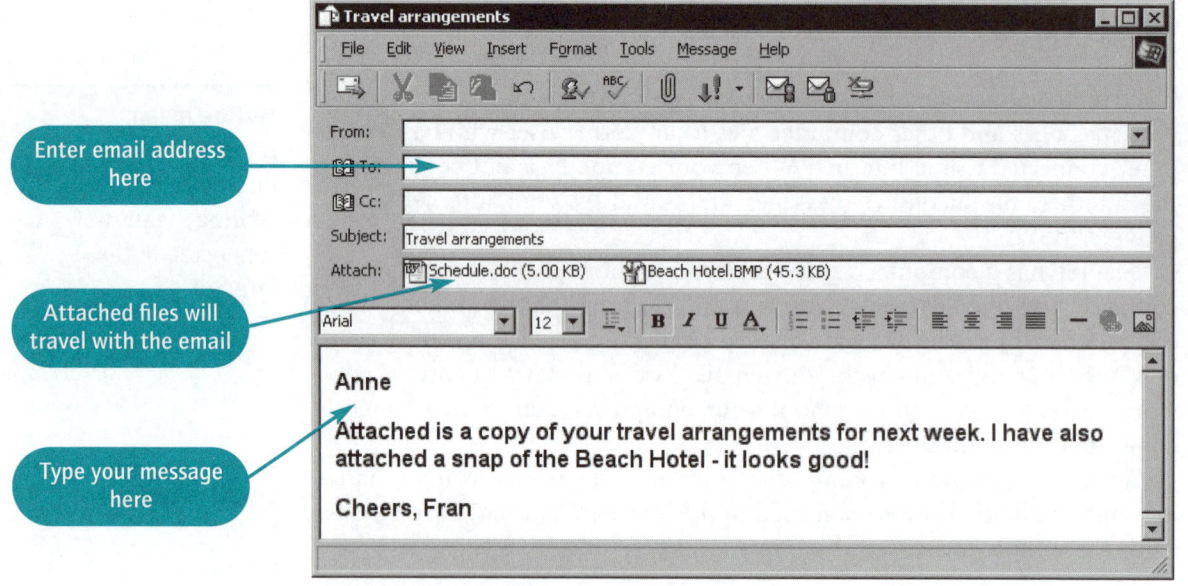

Creating an email with attachments

COMPOSE YOUR MESSAGES OFFLINE

If you are paying for your connection time, it is best to write your messages offline, before you go online. You can then take your time and prepare several messages which are stored temporarily in your outbox. When you go online the email software can quickly send mail from your outbox and will get any mail which is waiting for you. New mail will appear in your inbox.

Sending email
- Select the command or icon for a new message.
- Use the **To** field to enter the email address you want to use. This address might be available from the address book icon at the top of the screen.
- Use the **cc** field if you are sending anyone a copy.
- Use the **Subject** box for your choice of short title.
- Use the body area to type your message. You can also use the paste command to import any clip art or other effects.
- To attach a file, use the appropriate command or icon then point to the place in your computer where the file is saved
- When finished, use the **Send** command. If you are online the email will be sent. If you are offline the email will be sent next time you go online

Receiving email
- Make sure you are online. For home computing this normally means selecting the icon of your internet service provider (ISP).
- The modem will dial your ISP and you may have to enter your password.
- Once you are online, use the appropriate command to download any messages from your mailbox held at the ISP.
- Any income mail is downloaded to your inbox; click on any new messages to open them.
- Read the message and perhaps reply by selecting **Reply**.
- Exit the message then transfer it from your inbox to a storage folder.

Email addresses

There are many millions of people on the Internet and there are many possible email addresses. You need to be careful when reading and writing an address you have been given. Although they may seem confusing, email addresses always follow the same pattern:

yourname@reallybigcompany.com

(user name → separator → domain name → dot → type of domain)

Types of domain

.com	commercial
.org	non-commercial
.gov	government
.edu	educational
.net	network
.co.uk	UK commercial

- **User name:** this is your personal address. It could also be two names separated by a dot such as jim.jones or an underscore such as mary_jones.
- **Separator:** found on your keyboard, sometimes called the 'at' or 'axon' symbol.
- **Domain name:** an organisation has to register their particular name.
- **Type of domain:** helps to indicate the type of organisation, such as business, government, network and educational.

COMMUNICATING | 37

Common email abbreviations

AFAIK   as far as I know
BBL   be back later
BTY   by the way
FAQ   frequently asked questions
IMHO   in my humble opinion
RTFM   read the flipping manual
TTFN   tat ta for now

Netiquette

Etiquette means good manners, netiquette means good manners on the net. If you are emailing a stranger it is wiser to be polite, just as you would with a letter or phone call. Some suggestions:

- Don't shout with capital letters.
- Always fill the **Subject** field with a helpful title.
- When replying, don't return the whole of a message.
- Check the address before you hit **Send** or **Reply**.
- Wait and think before you reply.

Messages can cause embarrassment if they reach the wrong people or fail to arrive with the right people. You cannot recall emails once they are sent.

Emoticons

:-)   happy
:-(sad
;-)   wink
:-0   shock

Presenting work

Computers can help you to show your work to other people, such as presenting the results of a project. The word processor, spreadsheet and graphics programs described earlier give you plenty of choices for making your work look good.

Whichever method you use to present your work, it is important to make a good impression. Here are some things you can do to check and improve your work:

- Check that the content is relevant – don't use it just because you have it.
- Select the important information and make sure it stands out.
- Put lots of space between items.
- Beware of using too many fancy effects.
- Use a spellchecker then use a human being.
- Ask other people what they think.

Some presentations

covers for projects
text for projects
project results
announcements
financial information
marketing information
automatic slide shows

Presentation programs

Specialised programs, e.g. PowerPoint, are designed to help you make materials for presentations and then to run the presentations. You can use presentation programs for the following purposes:

- Create OHTs or slides
- Store OHTs and slides
- Run a slide show from a computer
- Fade in and out between slides
- Print paper copies of all slides
- Print summaries of slides

Most presentation programs work in the same general way and have the following basic features:

- **Design options** allow you to choose different styles of ready-made slide plus ways of laying out information and graphics.
- **Notes** provide information to go with the slides.
- **Clip art** can be added along with other pictures.
- **Graphs and charts** can be imported from other packages.
- **Edit commands** allow work to be changed using undo, cut, paste and copy.
- **View** generates different types of slide, summaries, speaker notes and handout notes.
- **Slide show** allows you to show the slides full-size on the computer screen or on a projector screen; there is the option to add timing and let the slide show run automatically.
- **Slide effects** include special effects as slides change and added sound effects.

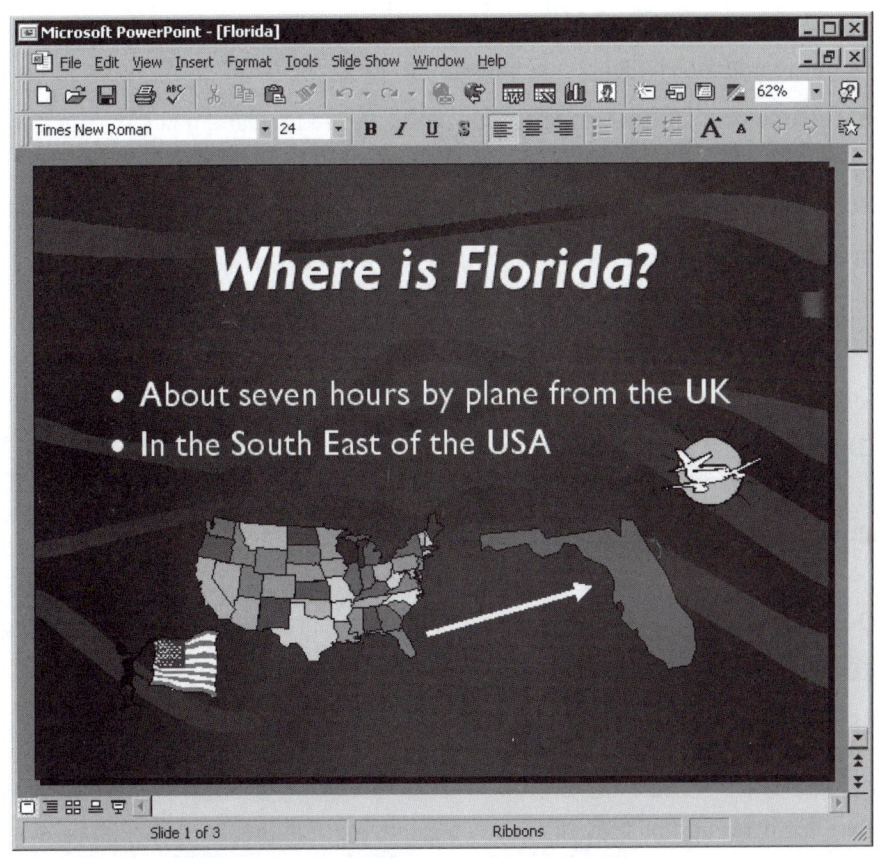

Typical presentation slide combining text and graphics

FORMAL DOCUMENTS: KEEP THEM SIMPLE

As the purpose of a document or a presentation becomes more formal, simple styles and effects become more appropriate.

COMMUNICATING | 39

Glossary

Alignment: arrangment of text compared to margins of paper. Left alignment starts each line hard against the left margin. Right alignment ends each line hard against the right margin (also called justified). Centred alignment places the text in the middle of the page.

Analogue: analogue data is represented by a quantity, such as voltage, which gets bigger or smaller depending on the size of the data.

Attachment: a file, such as text, that can be linked to your email message and will be sent with the email.

Bookmark: a shortcut to a favourite website; also called a favourite.

Browser: the software used to find and read websites on the Internet. Popular browsers are Microsoft Explorer and Netscape Navigator.

Clip art: drawings and other images you can import into your files.

Cookies: small text files placed on your computer when you visit some websites.

Digital: digital data is represented by combinations of fixed settings, e.g. combinations of 0 and 1.

Domain: part of a website address which shows where the site is from, e.g. .com or .co.uk.

Download: copying something from the Internet onto your computer.

EDI: electronic data interchange.

EFT: electronic funds transfer.

EFTPOS: electronic funds transfer at point of sale.

Email: electronic mail that allows you to send information to a particular person or computer connected to the Internet. Messages are stored centrally until you are ready to download them.

FAQs: frequently asked questions.

Flame: an abusive email.

Font: size and style of letters and other characters.

Home: the webpage your browser automatically points to when you log on.

Header and footer: the title at the top of a page and the page numbers at the bottom of the page which are repeated on each page of a document; they can be generated automatically.

HTML: Hypertext Markup Language is the standard format for creating and showing pages on the Web.

Internet: the huge computer network which links many smaller computers in the world to provide a huge system for information and email.

ISP: an internet service provider is a company that connects you to the Web and also handles your email.

Justification: *see* **alignment**.

LAN: local area network.

LCD: a liquid crystal display is a popular design on laptop computers.

Link: a word or picture that, when clicked, jumps you to a new place. Also called a hyperlink, it is usually underlined.

Macro: a pre-recorded routine or program which automatically carries out common tasks such as writing the date.

Mail merge: the automatic production of individualised letters using a database file.

Modem: a small box or plug-in card which connects your PC to the Internet over a phone line.

Offline: not connected to the Internet or other communications network.

Online: connected to the Internet or other communications network.

Pixel-based: produced by storing a collection of pixels (dots) to create a bitmap; *see also* **vector-based**.

Portal: a website which is designed as a first port of call and which has links to many other sites.

Query language: a set of words and symbols used to retrieve information from a database.

RAM: random access memory is part of the hardware in your computer which temporarily stores information. RAM is measured in megabytes (MB), e.g. 32 MB.

Ring network or loop: a way of connecting computers and a main computer via a ring circuit.

Search engine: a website site which finds other webpages when you enter keywords or ideas that interest you. Popular search engines are: AltaVista, AskJeeves, Excite, Lycos and Yahoo.

Server: a high-capacity computer which stores and distributes information such as webpages and email.

COMMUNICATING | 41

Software: the data which controls computer hardware and allows the computer system to provide services and information.

Spellchecker: an automatic routine which checks typed words against standard lists of words stored in the software.

Star network: a network where the main computer, or hub, is at the centre and has a separate connection to each computer.

URL: URL stands for uniform resource locator but is usually known as the website address.

Vector-based: described by coordinates such as the start and end points. May also be called line-based; *see also* **pixel based**.

WAN: wide area network.

World Wide Web: the part of the Internet which gives you access to the websites of organisations and people when you enter their web address in your browser.

WYSIWYG: what you see is what you get; the styles and layout on-screen will be the same on the printout.

Part 2: The Bottom Line

This part concentrates on what you must do to get your key skills qualification. It will show you:

- The words and ideas of the key skills.
- The definition of level 3.
- How you can practise the skills.
- What must be in your portfolio of evidence.

This part is divided into three sections:

- **What the unit expects:** This section will explain the evidence requirements of the IT key skill, and how to put your portfolio together. Your portfolio is the key to getting your key skill – this part of the book tells you how to choose your evidence and get it ready.
- **Evidence for level 3**
- **Other forms of assessment and evidence:** This section will tell you about the external assessment and how to prepare for it.

Qualifications and Curriculum Authority
The key skills specifications are published by the QCA, and are widely available through schools, colleges, training establishments and awarding bodies. They are also available on the QCA website (www.qca.org.uk).

What the unit expects

What is level 3 all about?

The key skill unit at level 3 asks you to show that you can apply your information technology skills and provide evidence in the following three areas:

- Planning and selecting information
- Developing information
- Presenting information

You can address each of the three areas individually to collect the rest of the evidence or, if appropriate, you can put together evidence that involves two of the areas together. Because of the amount of evidence you will need to produce, you will probably use all three ways of generating evidence.

One more key feature of the level 3 information technology requirements is that you have to do at least one **substantial** task that involves planning and selecting information, developing information and presenting information all together as part of the same task. You must do at least one task, but you could do more. Many of the signposts in Part 3 of the book highlight potential activities that are complex enough to help you meet this part of the evidence requirement.

You will find that regardless of what qualification you are doing, or what you might be interested in, there will be something that you will be able to identify as complex and substantial.

What's your point?

Your key skill is about using information technology to help you meet your aims or goals. It is not simply about IT in isolation, just you playing around with a computer. So it is not enough merely to find and present information using IT. You need to have a purpose for using the information you collect.

The IT key skills will keep asking you to use the information for a purpose, and you will need to provide evidence that you have a purpose in mind and you can use the IT effectively to meet it. Finding out information for a discussion, wanting to send some important message or information to someone quickly via the Internet, presenting your work in a report for an assignment, all are reasons for using IT. They are all purposes.

Evidence
Evidence is the proof that you can do what is required in order to get the key skill qualification. It is proof that you have learned about information technology and that you can use and apply what you have learned.

What about your portfolio?

Building your portfolio of evidence

Your portfolio of evidence is the work you have done to prove to your teacher and others that you can do what the key skills unit asks you to do. It is the proof you will need to get the key skills award.

A key skills unit is a respectable quantity of work, with the same credit as one Vocational A-level unit or one A-level module. Fortunately, you will already be doing this work in your other studies but you may have to carry out several different tasks to have sufficient evidence for the key skills requirements.

The successful operation of a computer application is very satisfying, but may leave little obvious evidence. You can spend many hours working on an automated presentation or webpage and, when it is working, one screen will just smoothly change into the next. So as you work you will need to think about what could be useful evidence. The two usual types of evidence are:

- A signed record by an assessor who saw you using the IT
- Printouts with suitable notes

The assessor will usually be your tutor, and if they are sure that your work is definitely your own work, they should be willing to sign you off. It makes their life easier if there is a prepared statement or form for them to sign.

For most requirements the main sources of evidence are printouts of your work at different stages, but especially before and after. This is a case where you should keep all your drafts and your mistakes, because changes are excellent evidence that you did develop the work. The printouts should be annotated with labels, brief notes and arrows pointing out stages, important features and changes. Presenting original printouts with your own writing is usually the best evidence.

Special factors e.g. disability
Alternative forms of evidence can be considered.
Ask your teacher or tutor for further information.

HINTS FOR ORGANISING YOUR EVIDENCE

- Have a contents page that you continually update as you collect your evidence.
- Keep records of when you collected your evidence and where it came from (e.g. which A-level or Vocational A-level unit).
- Get into the habit of writing down the purpose for your work as you collect evidence.
- Use the key skills sections (discussions, presentations, reading and synthesising and writing documents) to divide up your portfolio.
- Copies of work are acceptable if the actual key skills evidence is part of another course.
- Keep a checklist of all the things you must cover in your portfolio (e.g. in the presenting section you must show you can use an image).

THE UNIT EXPECTS | 45

Evidence for level 3

The key skill at level 3 is divided into three areas: planning and selecting information, developing information, and presenting information.

Planning and selecting information

What you must learn to do

Planning tasks
The requirement is to plan how you might obtain information for a substantial activity. You need to show you can use your planning skills to reorganise the large activity into a series of smaller, more manageable tasks and plan to do them in an appropriate sequence. This planning is needed for all three areas of evidence requirements: obtaining information, developing information and presenting information.

Different sources of information
You need to show that you can compare the advantages and limitations of different sources of information. The focus here is on your ability to make judgements about the suitability of different sources of information and your ability to assess the advantages and disadvantages of each. Your sources could include files on disk, CD-ROMs, databases, the Internet, emails, scanned information or any IT source.

See also: **Using databases**, page 12. **Using the Internet**, page 16.

Techniques to find information
Having shown that you can select appropriate sources of information, you need to show you can use appropriate search techniques to find the information you need. This might include using query techniques in a database or an Internet search engine. Some of these searches should involve the more advanced search methods such as multiple criteria which narrow searches, relational operators like < (less than) and logical criteria such as AND, OR, NOT conditions.

Making selections
When you have collected the information from the different IT sources,

you need to show you can sift out what will be important to include in your work. You need to show you can choose appropriate sources, but you also need to show you can be discriminating about the information you collect from them. To do this, you need to show you can use the two criteria of relevance and quality. In assessing the quality of the information, you may need to make judgements on the accuracy and reliability of the content. Reliability refers to whether the information will stand up to close scrutiny and whether it is dependable.

Collecting evidence

HOW TO GET YOUR EVIDENCE

What you need to do	*Business investigation*	*Population study*
You need to have two different purposes in mind, and then for each purpose: • Plan how to get the information you need to meet your purpose. • Search for the information you need by choosing appropriate sources and ways to find the information. • Use relevance and quality as a way of choosing what information you will use.	An extended business studies project consisting of an investigation of a particular business area, the generation of a proposal for a new business in that area, and the presentation of the results to a group. **Planning** I will be using information from a variety of sources with possibilities noted below. This wide brief has several major targets which might be considered as two different purposes needed for the key skill. I intend to use many aspects of this project to generate evidence for the key skill. Some activities will be group work but I will take care to keep careful records and clearly identify my own contributions. The project lasts for several months and falls into a number of stages. I will use an electronic diary to show my stages and to check progress. **Possible sources** **Texts:** information about company performance, business sector analysis and economic theory, company reports	Course work or an essay about the demographic trends of population in a given area. Subjects with an interest in this topic include history, geography, health and social care, construction and the built environment. **Planning** I will gather information from a variety of sources such as those noted below. Some sources are paper-based and in forms difficult to copy. The Internet and other IT sources can save travelling but I will need to decide if sometimes I should see an original, or obtain a paper copy. At the moment this information is for only one purpose but the figures might be useful in a later project. This topic deals in figures from databases, so it is a good opportunity for my IT evidence and for my Application of Number key skill. **Possible sources** **Texts:** textbooks and journals about population change, government information, local authority records, census results

CD-ROMs: archived reports, business databases

Internet: newspaper business articles, share prices and trends, company websites

Scanner: to capture useful non-electronic materials

Email: information from other people

Selection

I will need to be careful about:
- Opinion and bias, especially in company materials and from columnists
- Accuracy, currency and relevance of the information
- Copyright of information

Possible techniques

I will try to show use of IT techniques such as:
- Search for company figures greater than or less than certain values
- Search for companies with one aspect but not with another
- Saving results onto disk in an organised way
- Printing out, when needed
- Working safely

Continued on page 50

CD-ROMs: archive materials such as census results, geographic maps

Internet: government websites with statistics, university websites with links to sources

Scanner: to capture useful non-electronic materials

Email: information from other people

Selection

I will need to be careful about:
- Opinion and bias from textbooks and journals
- Accuracy, currency and relevance of the information
- Copyright of information

Possible techniques

I will try to show use of IT techniques such as:
- Search for data between certain years
- Narrow the parameters of a search by excluding certain areas
- Saving results onto disk in an organised way
- Printing out, when needed
- Working safely

Evidence requirements in a nutshell

You need to be doing a substantial activity and the subjects you are studying should demand this anyway. The tasks in the activity need to satisfy the key skills requirements; you may need to think about that. You have to be looking up different sources of information and using them for at least two different purposes.

When searching for information from databases or Internet sources, you need to show that you are effective. This is usually done by using good query techniques that produce a reasonable number of useful results instead of hundreds of general results. At all times you need to be critical and only select information which is accurate, unbiased and appropriate to your purpose. Consider how your use of IT compares with other ways of collecting the information.

Most of your evidence will be printouts and notes from your activities. Besides the information you have chosen as relevant, you need to provide evidence of how you worked, e.g. working drafts, rejected materials with annotations, notes about the sources and search methods used. Reality is more important than neatness.

See also: **What about your portfolio?** page 45.

> **HINTS ON PLANNING AND SELECTING INFORMATION**
> - When you are creating your plan, write down how you will use the information when you collect it.
> - Keep separate portfolio records for each of your two different purposes.
> - Show evidence of your planning by recording it – with IT of course. A table of project stages and dates in a word processor is a good start.
> - To show extra evidence of your IT skills, use project planning diagrams such as Gantt charts.

Developing information

What you must learn to do

Entering and combining information
This requirement asks you to assemble your information in a consistent form, which might include using lists, tables, spreadsheet grids and other ways of dealing with information in a regular way. Where relevant to the task, automated routines can include macros in word processors, mail merge routines, slide shows and any other prepared routines.

Using structures and procedures
This is looking to see whether you can use IT techniques to develop your initial information. These techniques can include sorting and grouping information, sending a mail merge, analysing numerical data using spreadsheet formulas, and generating graphs and charts from your data.

Exploring and deriving new information
This requirement is about using your IT to follow lines of enquiry. For example, changing a value in a spreadsheet to investigate its effect. Having used the IT to get new information you need to decide which result is the best for your purpose.

Exchanging information
Exchanging information and ideas needs to be part of your plans and obviously you should use IT. Methods can include email, sharing documents, using common templates and planning sheets.

See also: **Spreadsheets**, page 22; **Word processors**, page 27.

Collecting evidence

HOW TO GET YOUR EVIDENCE

What you need to do	*Business investigation* Continued from page 48	*Holiday planning*
You need to have two different purposes in mind, and then for each purpose: • Enter information and bring information together. • Use structures and procedures to develop text, images and numbers and to produce new information. • Use effective methods to exchange information to support your task.	An extended business studies project consisting of an investigation of a particular business area, the generation of a proposal for a new business in that area, and the presentation of the results to a group. **Entering and gathering information** The business figures that I have selected in the previous stage can be entered into a spreadsheet. **Developing new information** I can enter formulas in the spreadsheet to analyse the performance of the business data. These analyses can also be displayed as graphs. I can cut and paste headings and formulas from a spreadsheet and make some projections for a proposed business. I can test for best case and worst case. **Exchanging information** I am already exchanging with other members of the group by email. We are sharing a schedule for the progress of the project. **Possible techniques** I will try to show use of IT techniques such as: • Formatting text and adding labels • Using prepared templates • Copying into spreadsheets • Entering formulas • Calculating and checking results	Holiday planning for customers. I have already looked up the details of different holiday destinations popular with customers. I have climate statistics, hotel features, airline flight times, and costs of holiday packages. **Entering and gathering information** I can start a table and enter the destinations, airline choices and costs in separate cells. These can also be converted to a formal database if the project grows. **Developing new information** The temperature and rainfall statistics already exist in tables, so I can import them into a spreadsheet. The data on the spreadsheet can be sorted into categories. I can select data on the spreadsheet and produce a climate chart for a particular destination. I can use formulas in the spreadsheet to display holidays which match criteria such as price range and climate range. I can program the mail merge program to automatically send clients details of holidays which match their interests. I can use find commands to rapidly find data.

- Sorting items
- Selecting appropriate graphics

Continued on page 53

Exchanging information

Some airlines and holiday charter companies will email me with quotations for combinations not quoted in their standard information.

Possible techniques

I will try to show use of IT techniques such as:
- Search for data
- Use prepared templates
- Copy into spreadsheet
- Enter formulas
- Calculate and check results
- Sort items
- Select appropriate graphics

Evidence requirements in a nutshell

Earlier in your tasks you will have selected information from various sources. You now need to gather this information together in one place such as a list, table, database or spreadsheet. When the information is in this form, you can develop it by sorting, analysing and converting to other displays such as graphs.

You should use IT tools to explore your data and produce new information. For example, you can explore numbers by using formulas to find a maximum, a mean or some other average. With spreadsheets you can easily test different possibilities and justify conclusions.

As you develop your information there are many opportunities to show your IT skills. Make sure that you keep evidence of the different stages of work and don't throw away your experiments. This is usually a good time to show that you are using IT to communicate with other people, and at this level you should be working accurately and checking your work. You should also be using IT correctly and be aware of computer viruses and other system hazards.

Most of your evidence will be printouts and notes from your activities. In addition to your new information you need to provide evidence of how you worked by providing working drafts, rejected materials with annotations, notes about techniques, etc. Reality is more important than neatness.

See also: **What about your portfolio?** page 45.

> **HINTS ON DEVELOPING INFORMATION**
>
> - You can make a screenshot of your computer display at any stage to show evidence of your work in progress.
> - Press the **Print Screen** key; this captures the current screen onto the clipboard.
> - Open a new document in your paint program or advanced word processor.
> - Paste the screenshot into the document.
> - Make any relevant annotations then print it out.

Presenting information

What you must learn to do

See also: **Changing formats**, page 29.

Structuring your presentation
There are several things you can consider as you develop the structure of your presentation with features such as style of type, paragraphs and spacing on the page. You may need to adapt the templates that give standards styles. You need to think about how you are using reference features such as automatic page numbers and dates, and to use a sensible system of file names and draft numbers.

Consider asking people to give you feedback on the effectiveness of your proposed presentation, on your content, your layout, and any other relevant features.

Developing presentation
There are several ways to refine your work, making it look more impressive and giving it a greater impact on the reader, and information technology makes it far easier to try them out. Consider changing formats or layouts, overlaying images on texts and combining information.

Presenting information
You need to show that you can present information in a way that suits your audience and your purpose. You need to consider the merits of different options for presentations, e.g. paper and IT as well as monomedia, bimedia and multimedia presentations. Then you need to decide which would be the most appropriate.

Accurate and sensible work
There are various techniques to keep your work accurate: proof-reading, spellchecking and producing drafts so others can comment on them. Continually review your work, keeping in mind your original purpose and your intended audience.

Collecting evidence

HOW TO GET YOUR EVIDENCE

What you need to do	Business investigation Continued from page 51	Design presentation
You need to have two different purposes and audiences in mind, and then for each purpose: ● Make sure your work is correct and makes sense. ● Include at least one example of text, images and numbers.	An extended business studies project consisting of an investigation of a particular business area, the generation of a proposal for a new business in that area, and the presentation of the results to a group. **Developing structure** I have already developed my business plan using spreadsheets, charts and graphs. I can assemble them in a document and print them out in several different formats, e.g. a document and a slide show. I can show these draft results to different people, find out what they don't understand, and choose the best format. **Developing presentation** I will change the size and and layout of the trial presentations and prepare at least two different types of presentation. One will be a document, the other might be slides. **Implications of IT** If necessary, I can answer questions about the advantages of using IT for this project, and I understand that I must observe copyright and confidentiality where necessary. **Possible techniques** I will try to show use of IT techniques such as: ● Modifying templates and styles ● Automatic page numbering ● Using a spellchecker ● Changing formats ● Mixing graphics and text	Presenting a technical design solution which meets a given brief. Subjects with a requirement like this include design and technology, engineering and manufacturing. **Developing structure** I have explored different design solutions and chosen the one that I wish to present. I will use the CAD system to produce different technical perspectives and ask others which are the most accurate and effective. **Developing presentation** I will add dimensions, titles and labels to the various CAD drawings. **Presenting information** I will assemble the drawings in different formats: ● Screen views ● Printouts ● Automated walk-throughs **Implications of IT** The CAD software is very powerful and saves hours of manual drawing. Plus it can produce effects I can't achieve by any other method. **Possible techniques** I will be able to show use of various IT techniques: ● Standard drawing formats ● Hatching styles ● Adding dimensions ● Changing perspectives ● Developing 3D views

The Bottom Line

EVIDENCE FOR LEVEL 3

Evidence requirements in a nutshell

In this final stage of collecting evidence for your IT key skills, you need to show that you can bring together the correct information in a structured way and use it to give a presentation which works effectively. The material must include text, images and numbers; it must be accurate and it must make sense.

Good evidence will be a record of your final presentation, including text, images and numbers. As in the other stages, you will need to show evidence of how you developed your presentation. For example, you need to keep working drafts, trial materials with annotations, notes about software and techniques.

> ### HINTS ON PRESENTING INFORMATION
> - You can make a screenshot of your computer display at any stage to show evidence of your work in progress (see the box on page 52).
> - Rehearse your presentation aloud, especially if you have a limited time. Most presentations need pruning at rehearsal.
> - What will you do if your chosen IT equipment fails? Consider having a backup presentation.

Other forms of assessment and evidence

External assessment at level 3

You will need to take an external assessment as well as produce a portfolio of IT evidence. The external assessment is designed to show that you can work with IT at the correct level under a different set of circumstances. There will be a time limit, such as three hours, and you may be allowed to do it in a single long session or in several shorter sessions. This is up to your school, college or assessor to organise for you.

What is the point of an external assessment?

The idea of an external assignment is that someone else sets you a series of related tasks in information technology and gives you all the data and instructions needed to get on with the tasks. Doing the assessment provides evidence that you can apply your information technology in order to complete tasks set by other people.

Here is how to look at it:

- The portfolio shows that you can set your own information technology tasks and you can meet your own deadlines and time constraints.
- The external assessments show that you can carry out larger tasks set by other people and also meet the flexible time constraints that have been given to the tasks.

When you meet these requirements, you will get your key skill in Information Technology, and you will have proved that you can use IT under a range of different conditions and in different contexts.

Part 3: Opportunities

This part highlights opportunities for generating IT evidence in the qualifications you are taking. It will show you:

- How your qualifications can be used to generate IT evidence.
- Where the best opportunities for this evidence arise in the qualifications.

This part is divided into three sections:

- **Evidence from A-level courses:** You will find this section useful whichever awarding body you are with.
- **Evidence from Vocational A-level courses:** This section will be useful regardless of whether you are working towards a 6-unit or 12-unit award.
- **Information sources:** This section includes a selection of websites which you can use as starting points for research and evidence gathering on the Internet.

The examples provided should be seen as starting points for generating evidence. You will see that some qualifications provide more opportunities than others. However, all contain some opportunities and will at least get you started. Make sure that you take time to read not just your subjects but also subjects that are related to the ones you are taking. This will help you gain a fuller understanding of how and where number evidence can be produced. For example, if you are doing a Business GNVQ then look also at the Business Studies GCSE and the Retail and Distributive Services GNVQ. You may also want to check out the Leisure and Tourism GNVQ.

Vocational awards

The GNVQ Advanced awards are now called Vocational A-levels. From September 2001 GNVQ Foundation and Intermediate awards are likely to be known as Vocational GCSEs.

Evidence from A-level courses

Art A-level

About the syllabus
The Art awards aim to combine intellectual and creative development with analytical, experimental and technical skills. They are also intended to help you develop aesthetic understanding and critical judgement. The programmes of learning associated with these awards are intended to provide you with an appreciation of the interconnectedness of art, craft and design and their roles in different societies and cultures, both contemporary and historical.

See also: **Art and Design Vocational A-level**, page 86.

Topic area 1
Opportunities for evidence

Planning and selecting information
The production of a 3D outcome is a substantial and complex activity that will need to be broken down into a series of tasks. As you prepare to work in three dimensions, you will need to plan and prepare. This will involve:

- Deciding on the focus of your research, including the media and materials you will use and the technology and equipment you will need.
- Looking at the appropriateness and relevance of different sources of information.
- Selecting appropriate techniques for finding information; in IT these will include Internet search engines and the range of multiple criteria.

The objects or artefacts that you produce will depend upon the quality of your exploration and research. Make sure the selections you make are based on their relevance to your purpose and the quality of their contribution.

Developing information
The images of other people's objects and artefacts you discover through IT are intended to:

- Help you discuss and evaluate 3D forms.
- Develop and extend your study of 3D forms.

- Provide you with potential lines of enquiry into media and techniques.
- Extend your understanding of making objects and artefacts and cause you to modify and develop your plans and ideas.

IT will enable you to:

- Bring together a range of information on different images and ideas in a consistent format.
- Use appropriate structures and procedures to record observations, ideas and insights.
- Explore the information and develop ideas by following lines of enquiry; develop visual language.
- Use appropriate software to model the information and derive new visual information. This may involve using computer-aided design to explore 3D imagery and to consider ideas, objects and artefacts in the round.
- Consider the views of others by providing them with electronic versions of your ideas to consider, e.g. through PowerPoint presentations or emailing requests with appropriate attachments.

Presenting information

IT may provide only a developmental role in producing the finished object or artefact. Its contribution will be:

- Generation of initial ideas
- Development of ideas through drawings or plans
- Collection of other people's views or collaborative working

Any presentation of finished outcomes will require the support of developmental work to clarify your ideas or your selection of information, research and analysis. Make sure the presentation of your work suits its required purpose by being:

- Accessible to others and clearly referenced, saved and recorded
- Visually stimulating and supportive of your ideas and outcomes
- Accurate and clear

IT may also provide the final outcome in the way that models or maquettes are often used to represent or project towards finished work. In these circumstances make sure that visual work is supported by:

- Text that explains the materials and processes to be used
- Numerical data that identifies the scale of the finished piece together with the costs and time lines for production

Topic area 2
Personal studies and investigations

Personal studies and investigations give you opportunities to do what you want with the media and materials you want to work with using the techniques and technology that interest you.

Planning and selecting information

As with any extended project, you will have to plan carefully and this can best be done by breaking down your project into a series of discrete tasks. These should include:

- Looking at the range of sources and deciding which are most suitable for your purpose
- Choosing and using IT to collect and record information
- Confidently and perceptively selecting information that will support your work

Developing information

Remember that not all information has to be electronically based in the first instance. You can add to information that has come from CD-ROMs and the Internet:

- Scanned images from magazines or your own visual records
- Direct drawing using software packages or electronic pens and tablets

IT can be used to:

- Combine and record visual ideas from different sources
- Sort and sift relevant images and ideas
- Develop and manipulate images and ideas as part of your creative development
- Explore and analyse as you firm up your ideas
- Extend and evaluate your personal response
- Communicate and discuss your development with others

IT offers you an innovative way to:

- Record your creative development
- Complete extended developments in a short space of time
- Explore the versatility of your ideas in different contexts
- Adapt or amend your ideas in line with other people's comments, evaluations or recommendations

Presenting information

IT provides you with a structured means for presenting your visual ideas, records or outcomes. However, it does have limitations and if you use it as your sole means of communication, you must ensure that it clearly suits your intended purpose and audience.

Whatever role IT plays in your work, make sure your visual outcomes satisfy these three criteria:

- They can be easily accessed or retrieved by other people.
- They can be developed and refined to make them easily understood.
- They realise your intentions and clearly reveal your purpose.

What you must know
Part 1: The Learning Curve will help you with the knowledge you need.

What you must do
Part 2: The Bottom Line will help you with the evidence you need.

Further opportunities for evidence

Although 3D design and personal projects are explored in detail here, the processes and methods are equally relevant to other specialist areas covered by Art A-level specifications, including:

- Fine art
- Graphics
- Textiles
- Photography

Biology A-level

About the syllabus
The Biology award aims to develop essential knowledge and understanding in biology and how to apply them in new and changing situations. It will also help you develop an understanding of scientific methods and the contribution of new technology, particularly information and communication technology. The programmes of learning will also help you to recognise the role and responsible use of biology in society and they will sustain and develop your enjoyment and interest in biology.

Topic area 1
Working on your experimental skills

Planning and selecting information
You will have the opportunity to formulate a clear and accurate plan, which will mean taking the experimental activity and breaking it down into a series of tasks.

You are expected to develop your biology skills by using IT. This will require you to identify the advantages and opportunities provided by the technology. These will always include:

- Accessing a range of different sources of information and knowledge
- Accessing the most up-to-date and relevant information and knowledge to help you identify and define a problem
- Exploring the range of appropriate apparatus and materials to investigate the problem
- Finding information on the measurements and observations likely to generate useful and reliable results
- Providing the opportunity to set up criteria to help you select information and knowledge relevant to your experiments and investigation

See also: **Health and Social Care Vocational A-level**, page 96; **Science Vocational A-level**, page 113.

Developing information
Your information will come from a range of sources and in a range of forms. These will include:

- Text-based information, including other people's ideas and

descriptions of experiments and your own notes on materials, methods and ideas.
- Images and diagrams including drawings of apparatus and methods.
- Numbers and other statistical data, including your own measurements of materials and outcomes.

You will be expected to enter and bring together information from a range of sources and use IT for these purposes:

- Sorting information into a consistent form in tables, charts or layout.
- Creating or presenting combined information in a range of new forms or formats, including tables, charts and diagrams.
- Exploring the entered information; predicting and testing your hypotheses.
- Deriving new information then interpreting and evaluating it to reach and justify conclusions.
- Communicating your ideas or findings with others, using email or shared access to suitably saved and stored documents.

> Check out the **websites** listed on page 121.

Presenting information

Communicating the results of your experimental and investigative activities, using biological knowledge and understanding coupled with IT, will require you to select and use appropriate methods to illustrate findings, show trends and make comparisons.

You will have the opportunity to:

- Explore the range of presentation techniques, such as templates and text structures including different styles and formats.
- Increase the impact of your findings by combining text, images and numerical data to support your hypotheses.
- Present information in a range of different ways to meet the needs of different audiences and situations, e.g. an oral presentation and a final report.
- Check that your work is accurate and sensible; where spreadsheets are used, make sure any formulas are applied consistently and logically.
- Evaluate the implications of using IT with the techniques in your experimental work; recognise the strengths or weaknesses of the technology.

Topic area 2
Preparing for your practical examinations

Practical examinations will build on the experience, knowledge and techniques you have developed during your work on experimental skills. These examinations seek to determine how well you can carry out the process on your own. In preparing and practising for the exam, you will have the opportunity to develop a range of skills that will generate authentic evidence for your IT key skill.

The basic framework for experimenting and practical work is very similar to the structure of the IT key skill unit. You will need to plan and use different sources to search for and select information by breaking this process down into tasks:

- Plan a testable hypothesis
- Explore apparatus and procedures
- Select the number and type of measurements

Developing information

Any practical work will produce results that should be recorded in a form which can be analysed, interpreted, explained and communicated in a way that justifies your original hypothesis. This process will include:

- Analysing evidence to explore, develop, exchange and derive new information
- Ensuring measurements and observations are accurate and reliable by bringing together information in a consistent form
- Presenting observations and calculations to make predictions and test hypotheses
- Identifying trends and patterns by doing calculations and making deductions

Presenting evidence

Practical work will produce a range of different information, including text, images and numbers, that will record details and conclusions from experimental data. Here are some points to consider in the evaluation:

- Critical analysis of experimental techniques may gain more visual impact by changing the format or the layout.
- Charts, diagrams, graphs and tables should present information so it meets its purpose.
- Trends and patterns should be explained to meet the needs of the audience.

The critical analysis should show an awareness of the benefits and disadvantages of IT. This will include the contribution it has made and how it has influenced your practical work. You may also wish to suggest how further investigations will provide additional evidence to support your hypothesis or extend your enquiry.

Further opportunities for evidence

The Biology A-level has specific requirements for IT. When taking forward your studies in biology, you will have a range of opportunities to generate additional key skills evidence.

What you must know
Part 1: The Learning Curve will help you with the knowledge you need.

What you must do
Part 2: The Bottom Line will help you with the evidence you need.

Business Studies A-level

About the syllabus

The Business Studies award aims to develop an understanding of organisations, the markets they serve and the process of adding value. It will help you to understand business behaviour from the customer, manager, creditor, owner and employee perspectives and it will improve your own decision-making and problem-solving skills. This subject can provide you with the opportunity to plan and carry through the substantial activity required by the key skill at this level.

See also: **Business Vocational A-level**, page 89; **Retail and Distributive Services Vocational A-level**, page 111.

Topic area 1
Marketing

Planning and selecting information

You will need to understand how a business behaves as it looks to find then satisfy customers. The planning skills you develop will include:

- Setting objectives relating to individual tasks
- Deciding where to seek information, including electronic forms
- Choosing appropriate techniques for finding information such as Internet search engines
- Selecting and interpreting information that is relevant to your activity

You must make sure that the methods and sources you use provide you with accurate, reliable and relevant data and information. You will be expected to find information on:

- The market for your chosen businesses
- The market research techniques used by your chosen businesses
- The marketing planning used by your chosen businesses
- The accounting and financing processes that underpin marketing

The way you organise the collection and selection of data may be influenced by the market research techniques used by your chosen business.

Developing information

In carrying out your market research, you will have a wealth of information in a variety of forms, including hardcopy information from reference books or reports and electronic information such as:

- **Text**: including collection methods such as questionnaires.
- **Images**: such as charts and diagrams.
- **Numerical**: such as spreadsheets or graphs.

For this information to be meaningful and usable it must be:

- Entered and brought together in a consistent form
- Sorted and grouped
- Saved in appropriate directories, files and references

You will need to analyse the information and follow lines of enquiry to confirm your understanding, explore your ideas and test out your theories. To do this you may wish to:

- Change the form of the information, e.g. tables of statistical data into graphs
- Use formulas in spreadsheets to test out new ideas
- Use email or shared access to documents to work collaboratively with others

Presenting information

Your understanding of market behaviour will depend upon the range of sources you access, the quality of the information they provide and your ability to understand, evaluate and develop the information you find.

Your ability to communicate your findings will affect how others judge the quality of your work. IT has a particularly important role to play in effective communication and presentation, both oral and text-based. This should be much more than mere word processing:

- You should develop your presentation to suit your subject and your audience.
- You should present information in its most appropriate forms, such as:
  - text to explain the nature and role of marketing
  - images, including diagrams and charts, to represent the information you have collected
  - numbers, in tables and graphs, to quantify the information you have collected
- You should check that what you present is accurate and makes sense to others.

Check out the **websites** listed on page 120.

Topic area 2
Accounting and finance

Planning and selecting information

You will need to demonstrate how accounting and financial information are used to assist decision making and financial control in business organisations.

IT can help you to identify sources of information on:

- Different financial techniques, including:
  - budgeting
  - balance sheets
  - profit and loss accounts
  - classification and analysis of costs
  - investment appraisal
- Appropriate software and automated routines that will enable you to use the technology to manage, record and evaluate business performance.

EVIDENCE FROM A-LEVEL COURSES | **65**

Make sure that the techniques you select match the purpose of your investigation. You should discuss your selections with your tutor or others working with you on this topic to confirm your own judgements.

Developing information

You are not expected to produce your own information or accounts but you are expected to modify the accounts of others and, where relevant, to assess profitability and liquidity. This will require you to enter and bring together numerical information in a clear and consistent form.

You will need to sort and group information. You may wish to use a spreadsheet to explore the numerical information you have collected. This may include:

- Using spreadsheet formulas to make predictions and test hypotheses
- Converting numerical information into graphs or charts
- Calculating gross and net profit
- Demonstrating the relationship between costs and levels of output

IT provides you with the opportunity to work collaboratively with others through shared access to centrally saved files or by exchanging ideas and information using email with attachments.

Presenting information

The central purpose of accounting and finance is to ensure that business decisions are made in the light of the strategic objectives of the business and are shaped by financial information and data.

Your work on this topic should show that you understand:

- How budgets and finance are used for income and expenditure
- The differences between cash flow and profit
- How to interpret a balance sheet and profit and loss account

Your use of IT will help you to select and develop the most appropriate presentation of your understanding. You will use text, images and numbers to combine qualitative and quantitative information. These should include considerations of:

- The impact of format and layout
- The balance of text, images and numbers
- The role of multimedia presentations (PowerPoint)
- The nature of your audience

The extent to which your work on this topic is successful will depend upon the accuracy and relevance of your findings on accounting and finance, and the appropriateness of your use of IT in comparison with other available systems.

What you must know
Part 1: The Learning Curve will help you with the knowledge you need.

What you must do
Part 2: The Bottom Line will help you with the evidence you need.

Chemistry A-level

About the syllabus

The Chemistry award aims to develop essential knowledge and understanding in chemistry and how to apply them in new and challenging situations. It will also help you to develop an understanding of the connection between theory and experiment and how advances in information technology and instrumentation are used in chemistry. The programmes of learning will help you to appreciate the responsible use of scientific knowledge and evidence in society and they will sustain and develop your enjoyment and interest in chemistry.

Topic area 1
Applying your knowledge and understanding

Planning and selecting information

You will be expected to recognise, recall and understand facts, terminology, principles, concepts and practical techniques. This is relevant information you must draw on as you plan a substantial activity in chemistry.

IT provides you with a range of relevant sources including:

- Databases of chemical information
- The Internet and its many websites
- CD-ROMs on general and specific topics
- Files on disk of other people's research
- Scanned material

You will need to identify and choose appropriate techniques to find and sort information. This will include:

- Database query techniques
- Internet search engines
- Multiple criteria
- Logical criteria

You will need to make selections based on their relevance to your topic or projects and you will need to differentiate between important and extraneous material.

A recognised source of information is the periodic table, which records elements and their compounds. This source will provide you with an opportunity to demonstrate an ability to select relevant information, translate it from one form into another and record it in an appropriate format.

Developing information

Opportunities will naturally arise throughout the course when you will need to order, combine and sort information and data. IT offers you an opportunity to create lists and tables and use other people's automated routines to bring this information together in a consistent format.

See also: **Science Vocational A-level**, page 113.

Once you have entered and brought together your factual knowledge, you will be expected to recognise and show an understanding of specific chemical facts, terminology, principles, concepts and practical techniques. IT can be used to explore and develop this information, allowing you to extend your understanding and communicate it to others.

Chemical information can be:

- Interpreted and translated from tables into graphs, etc.
- Used to develop lines of enquiry involving calculations or fomulas
- Used to assemble and analyse experimental findings
- Used to make predictions, test hypotheses and refine models
- Shared with others for confirmation or constructive criticism (via email or on websites)

Presenting information

Assessing the validity of your chemical information, experiments and evaluations are fundamental skills. You will be expected to select, organise and present relevant information clearly and logically using specialist vocabulary. IT can be used to:

- Develop an appropriate structure for your presentation
- Select the appropriate forms, e.g. text, images, numbers
- Present information so it suits your project and your audience
- Use spellcheckers, grammar checkers and similar routines
- Seek the views of others to check your chemistry is understandable

Topic area 2
Working on your experimental and investigative skills

Planning and selecting information

You will be required to develop and plan an experimental and investigative activity. The IT key skill describes this as a substantial activity. This is best done by breaking down the activity into a series of tasks, each of which requires appropriate skills and techniques.

You will need to:

- Select appropriate sources of information, including electronic sources
- Demonstrate safe and skilful working practices on IT systems and in the laboratory
- Select appropriate techniques for locating information and doing investigative activities
- Be accurate, reliable and relevant when you record observations and select information

Developing information

Experimental and investigative work will provide you with qualitative (observational) and quantitative (measurement) data. You will be expected to know how to:

- Make observations and measurements with appropriate precision

- Record your qualitative and quantitative data in a consistent form
- Create structures that will help you interpret, explain and explore your data
- Derive new information, make calculations and organise your results
- Evaluate and communicate your results clearly and logically
- Use appropriate technology, including email with attachments or shared access to files

Presenting information

Your experiments and investigations will have produced:

- A set of qualitative notes
- A set of quantitative measurements
- Your interpretation of your findings
- Your evaluation of your methods

IT can support your presentation of these outcomes by:

- Structuring your presentation using established conventions, including automatic references such as headers, footers and pagination
- Selecting appropriate forms of text, images and numbers to increase the impact and understanding of your material
- Presenting information that suits your original problem
- Checking for accuracy and sense

You will need to be clear about why you have used IT systems and presentations. This will include the advantages gained as well as how you would make improvements in future.

What you must know
Part 1: The Learning Curve will help you with the knowledge you need.

What you must do
Part 2: The Bottom Line will help you with the evidence you need.

Computing A-level

About the syllabus
The course for Computing A-level will typically include the study and application of different methods of representing and processing numbers in computers. There will also be opportunities to work with data communications, networks, operating systems and a range of hardware and software.

As you are already doing a course in computing, it may seem easy and logical to gain the key skills unit in information technology. So it is, but you need to remember that the key skill is about *using* information technology to help you meet your aims or goals, not IT in isolation. It is not enough merely to find and present information using IT; you need to have a purpose for using the information you collect.

See also: **Information and Communication Technology Vocational A-level**, page 100.

Providing evidence

You also need to provide evidence that you can apply your information technology skills, at the correct level, in the following three areas:

- Planning and selecting information

- Developing information
- Presenting information

Part 2 of the book explains the requirements for evidence and suggests how you might capture evidence for each area. Level 3 also requires that you plan and carry out at least one substantial task using IT. You should therefore look at your course work or projects as a major opportunity to generate evidence.

Design and Technology A-level

About the syllabus
The Design and Technology awards aim to develop innovation, design capability, recognition of constraints and the ability to produce high-quality products. This award will provide you with the opportunity to select and apply knowledge, understanding and the skills of the design production processes to a range of technological activities. These programmes of study will provide you with the opportunity to develop a critical understanding of design and technology activities from contemporary and historical practices.

You will be expected to use a full range of knowledge, skills, understanding, attitudes and aptitudes inherent in design and technological activity, and to make informed choices about appropriate applications and uses. These skills are at the heart of key skills capability and confidence. Your work in design and technology requires you to use IT to enhance your capability. This provides you with the opportunity to develop and explore IT as a key skill.

See also: **Engineering Vocational A-level**, page 94; **Manufacturing Vocational A-level**, page 105.

Topic area 1
Product development (designing)

Planning and selecting information
The specialism you have chosen – product design, food, systems and control – will require you to undertake a design-and-make assignment. You will need to identify, explore and analyse a range of user needs and problems to generate sufficient information to inform the development of your design brief.

Each design brief should be seen as a substantial activity, which you will be expected to break down into a series of tasks. You will also be expected to compare the advantages and limitations of different sources of information with respect to IT and other tools. Information can be drawn from:

- Primary sources such as direct observation or consultation with others
- Secondary sources such as information from manufacturers, consumer organisations or other people

IT can support your collection of primary and secondary data:

- **Primary data**: IT helps you to produce data-handling or observation sheets and questionnaires.
- **Secondary data**: IT gives you access to other people's databases, files or websites, and this will help you develop awareness of industrial methods and approaches to design, manufacture and quality control.

Once you have collected the data, you must check for bias, relevance and sufficiency:

- Information should be reliable and unbiased.
- Information should be accurate and of good quality.
- You need to have enough information to begin your product design.

Developing information

You will be expected to generate and develop a range of design ideas and solutions. IT can contribute to this process by:

- Entering and bringing together your data in a consistent format
- Creating and using structures and procedures to develop and refine your design ideas and solutions
- Exploring a range of design ideas and solutions by changing values and rules in models
- Deriving and evaluating new ideas and information

Check out the **websites** listed on pages 121 and 123.

The contribution of IT to different aspects of design and technology will also include these aspects:

- **Product design**: the use of specialist drawing software.
- **Food**: the contribution of specific nutritional information in databases and spreadsheets.
- **Systems and control**: the understanding and analysis of circuit boards and peripherals represented in diagrams and drawings.

Presenting information

The strategies for developing, representing, evaluating and presenting your design ideas will need to be carefully chosen. You will be expected to communicate your ideas and information using text, images and numbers. IT can support your use of established design and technology conventions by using:

- Text to record and explain design decisions, including appropriate and accurate technical language
- Graphical techniques to represent or illustrate ideas and proposals
- Spreadsheets, tables and charts to present essential measurements, numerical or statistical information

Always make sure that IT is used to communicate your design information accurately and unambiguously to your chosen audience. This means that your use of IT should help others to make sense of your design proposals. You are advised to allow others to look at your work and provide you

EVIDENCE FROM A-LEVEL COURSES | 71

with feedback on content, layout, format, style and clarity before you carry out formal and final presentations. This will allow you to make all refinements necessary and secure effective and efficient communication.

Topic area 2
Product development (making)

Planning and selecting information

You will be expected to develop, produce or refine a production plan that will involve taking what may be seen as a substantial activity and breaking it down into a series of discrete tasks.

The main sources of information will be the original design specification and manufacturer and trade information relevant to the materials and equipment to be used. IT can be used to:

- Identify up-to-date costs of materials and components
- Explore computer-aided manufacturing methods
- Access the Internet for research information

To make best use of this information, you will need to have read and understood the drawings, tables and charts associated with product realisation and the relevance of other information to the design specification. This may lead you to revise the production plan or the equipment and materials required.

Developing information

You will be expected to bring together your information in a coherent form and, where appropriate, use ICT along with computer-aided design and manufacturing to:

- Design products
- Make accurate manufacturing drawings
- Determine quantities and costs
- Adjust estimates for different scales of production
- Understand automated production (computer-aided manufacture (CAM))
- Exchange information with other people
- Consider the accuracy and appropriateness of your work

Presenting information

You will be expected to present and evaluate outcomes. IT can support you in this process by ensuring that you:

- Use effective structures to communicate your outcomes
- Use text, images and numbers to show how you have achieved optimum use of materials and components
- Review the effectiveness of the work plan and present alternatives for future refinements
- Select and demonstrate methods for testing the performance of outcomes and products

Design and technology allows you to compare the contributions made by different IT systems. You may wish to comment on the advantages that IT offers in terms of production, communication, modelling and control.

Further opportunities for evidence

The topic areas designing and making should each provide sufficient evidence for the IT key skill. However, other projects requiring a full design-and-make activity may also provide opportunities.

The programme of study itself will provide many opportunities for you to develop your IT skills. Evidence for discrete tasks should be carefully recorded in order to provide supporting evidence for the more complex and extended activities.

What you must know
Part 1: The Learning Curve will help you with the knowledge you need.

What you must do
Part 2: The Bottom Line will help you with the evidence you need.

General Studies A-level

About the syllabus

The General Studies award aims to develop your ability to integrate knowledge from a range of disciplines. You will be required to demonstrate how this combined knowledge provides you with a greater understanding of the issues studied. You will learn how to interpret information and make informed judgements based on the evidence available. The programme of study will provide you with the opportunity to think constructively, critically and logically and explore a range of different approaches to problem solving. You will be expected to communicate your attitudes, ideas and solutions clearly and coherently using an appropriate format and style. The skills and knowledge you develop are at the heart of the key skills capability and confidence.

The key skill of IT is not a central requirement of the General Studies scheme of assessment. IT can be used as:

- A source of information as you seek to develop a greater understanding of human knowledge, understanding and behaviour.
- A process to help you integrate and organise information from a range of disciplines and to help you understand how they are interrelated.
- A tool for effective communication, especially in programmes of study containing course work.

Topic area 1
Application of mathematics

Preparing for your examinations
The General Studies award sets examinations in three overlapping areas:

- Science, mathematics and technology
- Culture, morality, arts and humanities
- Society, politics and the economy

EVIDENCE FROM A-LEVEL COURSES | 73

Each of these areas will require you to develop and extend your knowledge and understanding of the disciplines involved and how they interrelate.

In preparing and researching for these examination papers, you will need to plan and select information then organise and present it. These are the skills that comprise effective use of IT, so by practising and preparing for your General Studies examination, you can generate valid assessment evidence for the key skill.

Planning and selecting information

IT is an important source of information about attitudes, beliefs and ideas. Electronic information can be found on databases, CD-ROMs and the Internet:

- Databases contain lists of relevant topics
- CD-ROMs contain documentary evidence and other texts
- The Internet has specialist websites with the latest ideas

IT gives you access to a great deal of information, so you will need to be selective. Selection should be based on the relevance of the information to the topic or theme you are following and on your judgements about the quality of the information available. When you are dealing with ideas and opinions there is a likelihood of bias. You must approach bias with critical awareness and understanding.

You should always be aware that IT is only one of many sources of information. Think critically, logically and constructively about the implications of using it. Consider both the benefits and limitations of technology. Analysis of IT in this way will also help you to develop your own critical skills, which can be more widely applied to your programme of study.

Developing information

You are expected to be able to analyse and evaluate the information you select and be capable of exploring the implications. IT can support this by enabling you to:

- Combine and sort information into a consistent form that can be easily accessed.
- Organise information into text, images or numbers and translate readily from one form to another.
- Explore the information by following lines of enquiry and testing out hypotheses.
- Evaluate information from a range of different sources in order to make informed judgements and reach and justify conclusions.
- Exchange your ideas and conclusions with others by using email or other electronic facilities, in order to confirm or revisit them in the light of further views.

Presenting information

You will not have the opportunity to present your ideas or conclusions using IT during the General Studies examinations. However, as you prepare and research using IT you may wish to use it to help you organise and record your findings or outcomes in a way that will help you prepare and revise more easily. IT can help you to:

- Organise and save your research under appropriate file names and in accessible documents.
- Increase the impact of your research by enabling you to choose a format that makes revision or reading straightforward, such as the use of bullet points or headings and sub-headings.
- Compare and contrast attitudes, beliefs or ideas by using a layout that enables you to read across data in tables, charts or columns.
- Explore how to present information so it suits your purpose and helps you prepare future presentations for other audiences.

Topic area 2
Preparing for internal assessment

Planning and selecting information

You will be expected to undertake some personal research and to look critically at a wide range of sources. As you prepare and plan to undertake the assignment, you will need to break down this substantial activity into a series of discrete tasks. Each one should be clearly set out alongside its objectives and the means by which they can be achieved.

IT should be explored as a source of information. It can provide information online and offline:

- Disks and databases (offline)
- CD-ROMs (offline)
- The Internet (online)

You should also consider other non-electronic sources of information such as textbooks, manuals, magazines, newspapers and reports. The information you choose should be balanced, free of bias, relevant and reliable.

Developing information

IT can provide an accessible means to integrate information from a range of different sources. This may involve scanning in hardcopy as well as downloading information from the Internet. Comply with any copyright and confidentiality requirements and run a virus check when downloading files.

You will be expected to:

- Analyse the material and evidence you have collected
- Demonstrate a grasp of concepts and principles
- Show originality and problem-solving ability

IT can provide the means to:

- Sort and group your ideas and present them in text, images and numbers

EVIDENCE FROM A-LEVEL COURSES | 75

- Consider methods and theories that will help you to make predictions and test hypotheses
- Reach a conclusion that draws together information from a variety of sources
- Use email to confirm your conclusions with others and refine them in the light of their comments

Presenting information

You are expected to present a report that demonstrates intellectual depth and capability. The report should use a balance of text, images and numbers to support your conclusions and judgements.

Your approach to the report should be based on securing as much accuracy, clarity and precision as possible. IT is not a prerequisite, but it is recommended and it will enable you to:

- Reference your report clearly using automatic facilities such as headers, footers and page numbers, as well as file names and document versions.
- Explore different presentation techniques that will increase the report's impact, such as typeface and point size, graphics, diagrams and charts
- Ensure that your use of language is clear and that grammar, punctuation and spelling are accurate by using automated routines to check them.

Be aware of the advantages and limitations of IT over other tools. Make sure that your work fully benefits from IT by seeking the views of others throughout the process.

What you must know
Part 1: The Learning Curve will help you with the knowledge you need.

What you must do
Part 2: The Bottom Line will help you with the evidence you need.

Geography A-level

About the syllabus

The Geography awards encourage you to acquire and apply knowledge and understanding of physical and human processes, they develop an understanding of the interrelationships between people and their environments, and they help you to appreciate the dynamic nature of geography, the environment and resources.

See also: **Travel and Tourism Vocational A-level**, page 115.

Opportunities for evidence

Here are two of the main skill areas in the A-level specifications:

- Identify, select and collect quantitative and qualitative evidence from primary sources, including fieldwork and secondary sources.
- Organise, record and present this evidence.

Somewhere in all syllabuses these two areas will feature as necessary skills requirements, and information technology can play a significant role in both of them. There is the opportunity to design research instruments using IT, and to use IT to record and analyse the results. Secondary sources provide even greater opportunities to use information technology.

There may well be specific databases that you need to access, websites you need to contact or Internet searches that you need to undertake. Each provides a clear opportunity to address part of the IT key skill requirements. In particular, they meet the requirements to choose appropriate techniques for finding information (e.g. database enquiry techniques, Internet search engines, and logic criteria for your searches like AND/OR/NOT conditions) and to show you can use these techniques to carry out effective searches.

Project work and investigations

Your geography qualification may have up to 30% of the final grade determined by course work assessment. This is most often done in the form of one large investigation. Check the course work requirements in your particular syllabus; course work is an area that can generate large amounts of IT evidence and you should make the most of it. You could be expected to provide written work of up to 2500 words in length and containing maps, data, diagrams, tables or other ways of presenting geographic information.

Check out the **websites** listed on page 121.

Such a substantial and important piece of work needs to be carefully planned and presented, and you need to explore ways of developing the information it contains to present it to maximum effect. The project production process will also benefit if you can produce drafts at various stages of development for you to revise and for others to comment on. This all points to producing your environmental investigation on computer using IT to enhance the quality of your work.

The investigation would constitute a substantial activity that could break down into a series of tasks and could potentially include tasks for all three aspects of the key skill (planning and selecting information, developing information and presenting information). Whether or not you can generate evidence for the various parts of the key skill really depends on the topic you choose to study. So once you have an idea for your course work project, spend a little time planning how it could also generate evidence to meet the key skill.

It is worth taking time over your planning because it can be used as IT evidence. Some topics will suit Internet searches more than others, some will be more likely to generate statistics or numerical data more than others, allowing you to explore ways to develop and present this type of information. However, virtually every project can be used to meet the IT requirements on presenting information.

The IT requirements to check on clarity, spelling and grammar will help you develop better quality work and may help you avoid losing marks unnecessarily.

EVIDENCE FROM A-LEVEL COURSES | 77

Geography study areas

Here is a table of suggestions for generating IT evidence from your geography course. You need to check the geography syllabus you are taking and the particular subjects that you intend to study. It might be useful to make your own table, similar to this one, mapping out the IT opportunities that your course and course choices may provide. You could then refine and develop it with your teacher. This would help you get a better idea of where your evidence will come from and how it will build up to create your portfolio.

Geography	IT key skill	Some activities
Population	*Planning and selecting information* – Internet, CD-ROM, database searches *Developing information* – Spreadsheet work with statistics and census data	Population growth statistics Census data, e.g. official websites offering census data
Physical systems	*Planning and selecting information* – Internet searches to find websites that contain information and pictures from satellites or specialist weather sites *Developing information* – There is a great deal of electronic information available and there should be plenty of opportunities to explore and experiment	Geographical information systems (GIS) Satellite imagery Satellite tracking Global positioning systems (GPS) Ecology IT resources and websites Automated mapping technology Digital ground modelling (DGM)

What you must know
Part 1: The Learning Curve will help you with the knowledge you need.

What you must do
Part 2: The Bottom Line will help you with the evidence you need.

Geography as a discipline has come to rely heavily on all sorts of information and communication technology to understand, interpret, predict or forecast different aspects of the world. Computer modelling is used to gain a better understanding of population growth and urban development; satellite mapping and weather monitoring systems use space technology. These ideas have even found their way into computer games; Sim City is just one example. Learning about any aspect of the ICT innovations used in geography will give you an opportunity to reflect on the implications of using IT and how this has changed what we know about the world.

History A-level

About the syllabus

The History awards encourage you to acquire and communicate knowledge and understanding of selected periods in history. You will develop an understanding of historical terms and concepts, and you will explore the significance of events, individuals, issues and societies.

Opportunities for evidence

The history content involved in generating information technology evidence really depends on the topics you are studying. The section below tries to identify areas of historical knowledge, skills and understanding that should be present in your courses regardless of the topic areas you choose. This might give you ideas about how to generate information technology evidence regardless of the topic areas you study.

The following activities can be used to generate information technology evidence relatively easily:

- Finding historical sources, arguments and discussions to help you analyse and then make judgements and draw conclusions.
- Doing coursework or internal assessment; in some history courses the internal assessment component can be up to 30%.

Aims of history courses

The History A-level courses encourage you to acquire and communicate knowledge and understanding about selected periods of history. A great deal of emphasis is put on the ability to acquire and interpret historical sources of information and to explore the significance of events, individuals, issues and societies.

The IT key skill is about planning and using different sources to search for and select information It requires you to explore, develop and exchange information and derive new information. It also requires you to present information, including text, numbers and images. You can use the IT key skill as a way of supporting and improving your work and you can generate evidence through your history course that can be used in your key skills portfolio.

Key skill areas

Finding and interpreting information

This type of activity is really your best opportunity to address the IT requirement on planning and selecting information. There will be a range of ways to do this and you will be given textbooks, copies of secondary source material and a host of other types of information. Don't forget the Internet and CD-ROMs. Both represent two major opportunities to show you can use IT and generate appropriate key skill evidence.

CD-ROMs are used to store a range of historical material from photographs to newspapers. Check what is available and relevant to the historical period you study. Using this type of source means making final choices about the material you want to use, determining what meets your purpose and is of good enough quality; this selection work can also be used as key skill evidence.

Using the Internet allows you to search for and access relevant historical data and to reflect on the advantages and limitations of the Internet as a source of information. By learning how to use appropriate search engines and search techniques, you gain access to better quality and more relevant historical information as well as showing you know how to choose appropriate techniques for finding information. This will demonstrate that you can carry out effective searches.

Informal presentation of your history work
You may want to present some of your work or research to small groups as a way of getting feedback from others. IT can help you present your work effectively and can assist in helping you create appropriate methods for presentation of text, images or even numerical data. If you've been collecting statistics, you can use IT to convert them into graphs that get your point across.

Formal presentation of your history work
This is really addressing the opportunities to generate information technology evidence that exist when you do project or internal assessment work. Producing a major piece of historical research can be a great way of generating information technology evidence. The key skill can also teach you how to organise your work and present it clearly and effectively.

By using the project work as an opportunity to meet the IT requirement on presenting information, your history work will also improve. Working on the organisation and presentation of your history work will improve the general quality of the project. IT can improve the impact of your project, helping you turn it into a well-structured document.

You will also able to generate draft copies, allowing you to polish your work and see how it is developing. To meet the IT requirements, your work needs to be accurate and intelligible; use spellcheckers and grammar checkers. This will clearly benefit the overall quality of your history work and may stop you losing marks unnecessarily.

Mathematics A-level

About the syllabus
The Mathematics awards aim to develop your understanding of mathematics and mathematical processes in a way that increases your capability and confidence. The ability to reason logically and to generalise will help you to recognise how problems, tasks and situations can be represented mathematically and then resolved, refined or improved. You will be

---

What you must know
Part 1: The Learning Curve will help you with the knowledge you need.

What you must do
Part 2: The Bottom Line will help you with the evidence you need.

expected to extend your range of mathematical skills and techniques and apply them in increasingly challenging contexts as well as recognising coherence and progression across and within the subject. The ability to choose appropriate mathematical skills and techniques, apply them to real-world problems and explore them using IT is where your mathematical studies overlap with the key skill of IT.

Topic area 1
Application of mathematics

Planning and selecting information

You will be expected to develop planning skills that will require you to recall, select and use your mathematical knowledge to represent real situations. This will involve planning a substantial and complex activity by breaking it into a series of tasks.

IT offers you the opportunity to:

- Extend your access to mathematical facts, concepts and techniques
- Explore a range of techniques for finding information and use them to carry out effective searches
- Select relevant mathematical facts and concepts
- Understand the advantages and limitations of other sources of information

> Check out the **websites** listed on page 119.

Developing information

The information you identify will need to be entered and brought together in a consistent format. IT will help you to:

- Construct lists, tables and graphical images; analyse data and produce tabular or pictorial representations of data.
- Develop structures and procedures for building rigorous mathematical arguments or proofs; support them with data represented by text, images or numbers.
- Explore mathematical information by developing models to represent real-world problems and by changing values and rules to make predictions and test hypotheses.
- Derive new information from calculations and their results then use it to make predictions and comment on the setting.
- Analyse data, and produce tabular or pictorial representations of data.
- Share your findings with other people and check their understanding or interpretation of your data.

Presenting information

Interpreting and presenting your results and explaining how they represent a satisfactory solution to the original task or problem, are central to mathematics and IT at this level. As well as presenting your findings, you are expected to understand and explain the benefits and limitations of the technology.

IT will help you to:

- Draw together your evidence in a refined form

EVIDENCE FROM A-LEVEL COURSES | 81

- Present your results using text, images and numbers, to improve clarity and impact
- Communicate your conclusions so they suit your purpose and your audience
- Present alternative solutions when your results prove inconclusive
- Evaluate your strategies and make suggestions for further work or alternative approaches
- Check the accuracy and clarity of your work using spellcheckers and grammar checkers

Topic area 2
Statistics

Planning and selecting information

The extent to which you will need to generate, collect or obtain relevant information will depend upon the nature and context of your task. Class work activities are likely to provide you with immediate access to data, whereas course work and projects will require you to undertake data collection.

Data may come from direct observation, experimentation, questionnaires, simulation or from secondary sources. IT can be used to:

- Produce questionnaires, recording sheets and other documents to collect your data
- Find relevant information through database enquiry, Internet access or searching other people's files
- Make selections based on the purpose of your project, relevance to ideas and lack of bias

Developing information

The data you collect may come from a variety of sources. IT will help you bring together your data in a coherent form using lists, tables, frames and graphical images. Use automated routines whenever possible to check for viruses and ensure consistency.

Once you are satisfied with the quality of the data, you will need to manipulate it and carry out statistical calculations to further your project. IT can support this in several ways:

- Spreadsheets can analyse and interpret data
- Appropriate software can translate data into graphs and charts
- Modelling techniques can make projections and test hypotheses
- Formulas can calculate answers for you to think about

Presenting information

Statistical information is usually presented using graphical representation. IT can provide a straightforward means of translating data from one form into another. Given this ease of translation, you will be expected to ensure that:

- Your data is presented accurately and with precision

- Your presentation suits your audience and reveals your purpose
- Your graphical images are appropriate for your data
- Your graphs use appropriate conventions
- Your graphs refer to your original purpose
- Any inconsistencies or shortcomings are clearly signalled
- Your presentation considers some alternative approaches
- Your graphical approaches are clearly explained and evaluated

Always support your main findings and judgements with carefully referenced annexes. These annexes may include an evaluation of the benefits and limitations of using IT plus examples of the data-handling sheets and questionnaires you produced at the outset.

What you must know
Part 1: The Learning Curve will help you with the knowledge you need.

What you must do
Part 2: The Bottom Line will help you with the evidence you need.

Physics A-level

About the syllabus
The Physics awards aim to develop essential knowledge and understanding in physics and, where appropriate, how physics is applied. They will also help you develop a connection between theory and experiment, an appreciation of how physics is used, and an idea of how it has developed to the present day.

Topic areas
Using sources of information
Planning practical investigations
Gathering experimental data
Making calculations and developing data
Presenting results and drawing conclusions

See also: **Science Vocational A-level**, page 113.

Planning and selecting information
One of your activities needs to be substantial you need to plan your approach by breaking the activity into manageable tasks. Information technology is a natural tool for gathering scientific information, and the key skills unit focuses on using IT to select the most useful items. Here are some activities that will produce the required evidence:

- Obtaining information on physics topics from online and offline databases
- Obtaining physical data and other numerical information from online and offline databases
- Finding out about equipment and how to use it
- Planning your practical work
- Using IT interfaces to gather data from equipment
- Selecting suitable information from experimental data

Remember to keep evidence to show that you sometimes had a choice of search methods and information sources, such as different Internet sites,

EVIDENCE FROM A-LEVEL COURSES | 83

and indicate why you made a particular selection. Be able to compare the advantages and limitations of your methods and your information.

Developing information

To use your information and experimental data you will need to assemble it in documents with consistent and logical formats, e.g. tables and spreadsheet grids. The requirement to explore and develop the information should naturally arise from your need to do calculations, find trends and produce graphics. Here are some typical activities which can generate evidence for the key skills unit:

- Assembling data from database searches or from practical work
- Analysing data to give statistical information such as trends
- Making calculations to investigate physical theories
- Making calculations for practical investigations
- Changing values in mathematical models to test hypotheses and make predictions

When exploring your data you need to show how you tried different values or rules; you can generate evidence by keeping a few spreadsheet printouts that did not give good results. As part of your activities you also need to exchange information by using IT methods such as email or shared documents.

Presenting information

You need to use IT to present your results in an effective manner and also show evidence of how you developed your presentation. Physics investigations offer many IT opportunities to present findings using text, images and numbers in a variety of formats. Here are some activities:

- Explaining topics in physics
- Presenting statistics using charts and graphs
- Presenting steps of your calculations
- Presenting any calculations for practical investigations
- Varying parameters in mathematical models
- Showing how you tested hypotheses and made predictions

As you develop your presentation you should keep some earlier drafts to show how it has altered; perhaps you've improved the layouts. It is useful to ask other people to give you feedback on your drafts and possible presentation techniques; the key skill unit requires that your final presentation should suit its audience. The presentation needs to be technically correct and it also needs to make sense, so, check it carefully and give it a proofread.

Further opportunities for evidence

Most physics investigations provide good opportunities to collect evidence for the IT key skills unit. The organisation of the IT key skills unit into

---

Check out the **websites** listed on page 119.

What you must know
Part 1: The Learning Curve will help you with the knowledge you need.

What you must do
Part 2: The Bottom Line will help you with the evidence you need.

planning, developing and presentation is the same basic format used for an experiment or other scientific investigation.

The mathematical techniques used in your physics work should provide evidence of using various IT techniques, including advanced calculators, spreadsheet work, mathematical and graphing programs. The Internet is a rich source of information for physics knowledge and physics applications.

Evidence from Vocational A-level courses

Art and Design Vocational A-level

About the specifications

The Art and Design award studies topics such as working with materials; developing, exploring and recording your use of visual language; investigating, exploring and recording other people's use of visual language; working with materials, techniques and technology; and working to set briefs. It also includes course work, personal investigations and presentation of work.

You are not required to use IT to develop your art and design skills but you should be prepared to explore the potential of IT to:

- Increase your access to up-to-date information through the Internet
- Improve your presentational skills through word processing and other software packages
- Broaden the range of your design experience through CAD (computer-aided design) and other software packages

See also: **Art A-level**, page 58.

Topic area 1
Developing, exploring and recording visual language

Planning and selecting information

Investigation, exploration and interpretation are key activities in developing your 2D and 3D visual language. Before you are able to explore and interpret effectively, you need to have a clear understanding of what you are doing and where you are starting. The skills you will develop and use in this context are similar for both IT and art and design. They involve:

- Planning carefully by breaking down any substantial activity into a series of discrete tasks. This will mean allowing time for exploration and skill development as well as meeting deadlines and adhering to schedules.
- Preparing carefully by carrying out detailed research for information from a range of different sources and collecting relevant information in the form of text, images and numbers, as appropriate.

Developing information

IT can support your exploration of 2D and 3D visual language by:

- Giving you access to other people's work through CD-ROM packages and gallery websites.
- Enabling you to enter and combine images from a range of different sources, including scanned images and electronically generated drawings.

Electronically generated images provide you with the opportunity to investigate ideas and try out new techniques easily and quickly. You must ensure that:

- Original images are sorted, referenced and saved using established conventions
- The structures you use to manipulate and modify images are carefully recorded and available for future use
- You work safely and minimise any health risks
- You observe any copyright requirements and respect the confidentiality of other people's ideas and visual language

As your ideas move towards the final outcome, you will probably wish to seek the views of other people. IT provides you with the opportunity to explore and respond to other people's views through the use of email and attachments; it can also allow you to work collaboratively, either on-site or at a distance.

Presenting information

Presenting art, craft and design work is a natural part of the process of creative development. It is particularly relevant in the case of IT, which allows you to present work to a variety of audiences, in a variety of forms and in a variety of settings.

IT can provide:

- A supporting role by presenting initial ideas and developments
- An alternative solution by presenting ideas through electronic images
- A final solution by generating 2D and 3D outcomes and communicating them to others

If you choose IT as your main development tool, you must always control, understand and manipulate it to suit your needs. Using established IT routines as your only means of development can sometimes be more limiting than enhancing.

Topic area 2
Other people's use of visual language

Planning and selecting information

A central theme of the Vocational A-level is an appreciation of historical and contemporary practice in art, craft and design. When seeking historical and contemporary references, as well as professional practice, you will have the opportunity to consider the range of sources for this type of information and how to access them.

Traditional sources include:

- Text and reference books on art, craft and design
- Gallery guides and exhibition catalogues
- Magazine and newspaper articles

Increasingly, IT offers you the opportunity to access these traditional sources and more interactive and current information, including:

- CD-ROMs containing electronic text and reference material
- Websites of galleries, artists and collectors
- Electronic newspapers, magazines and research documents

To access the most up-to-date information and the most relevant sites, you will need to become familiar with appropriate and effective procedures for finding information. These will vary according to the electronic source involved but they are likely to include database query techniques and Internet search engines.

Your greatest challenge will not be finding information, but sorting and selecting relevant and reliable material. This cannot be done electronically; you will need to use your judgement to determine what is fit for purpose and what is biased. Remember that artists, craftspeople and designers can offer you only an opinion about their work, and commentaries are rarely without prejudice or bias. You are working in an area where ideas are more likely to be subjective than objective.

Developing information

When you have accumulated information from a range of sources, you will need to bring it into a consistent format. IT can help you do this. It allows you to use automated routines to save, reference and file your material so it can be easily accessed and retrieved.

Once you have decided what is useful and collected it in an accessible form, you are expected to:

- Develop your own ideas about other people's work or practice
- Draw conclusions about your findings
- Use your information to justify your conclusions
- Exchange ideas and conclusions with other people
- Decide on an appropriate format for presenting your material
- Acknowledge your sources and evaluate their contribution

The extent to which IT helps you do this will depend upon the access you have and the way that you use it.

Presenting information

Your work on this topic should result in a portfolio of your historical and contemporary references. Your records could use IT to:

- Scan other people's images then annotate and print them

- Produce an illustrated study that combines text and images effectively
- Develop your 2D visual language through your use of IT
- Provide printouts or disks of work in progress and finished items

You may not wish to provide all evidence for this topic using IT. You should use your developing skills and judgement to decide how IT and other tools make their most effective contribution to increasing your confidence and capability.

Further opportunities for evidence

You should understand from the previous topics that IT can make two major contributions to your creative development:

- As a source of information and a means of generating reports that combine text and images effectively
- As a creative tool that allows you to quickly explore, develop, manipulate, revise and record ideas

IT can also be regarded as an end in itself; an increasing number of artists and designers develop and present their work in virtual form.

All Art and Design units provide opportunities for you to explore your attitudes to IT and the skills you are developing. The resulting evidence can contribute to achieving your IT award.

What you must know
Part 1: The Learning Curve will help you with the knowledge you need.

What you must do
Part 2: The Bottom Line will help you with the evidence you need.

Business Vocational A-level

About the specifications
The Business awards study a range of topics; the compulsory units give you a broad understanding of some fundamentals and the optional units are slightly more specialised. Both optional and compulsory units can be used to generate evidence for the key skills award. It is worth learning a little bit about all the units you are likely to study. This will allow you to get a better idea of how you can build up your portfolio of evidence for the information technology key skill, identifying which units can be used to generate evidence for the different key skill demands.

Here are some suggestions for how to use compulsory units to create key skill evidence. This information is designed to help you start planning and collecting the key skill evidence you need.

Marketing

Planning and selecting information
The best opportunities exist when you are collecting primary and secondary market research data. You will be able to access information about marketing, market research reports and individual companies by using the Internet. You may also find useful information by looking up websites of market research companies like Mintel or specialist trade magazines. IT

See also: **Business Studies A-level**, page 64; **Retail and Distributive Services Vocational A-level**, page 111.

will also be useful in helping you prepare methods for collecting information and for entering and working on results.

Marketing databases will be useful for finding information on customer behaviour, helping to establish things like customer preference and buying patterns, sales trends and product substitution. There will also be opportunities to find out about market share, market segments and competitor activities. Searching this type of information source appropriately will help you generate evidence for the key skill requirement on planning and selecting information.

Developing information
You could use data analysis software, spreadsheets or other packages to develop your market research information. This will also give you an opportunity to calculate or deduce results and create new information.

Presenting information
Producing a marketing strategy can be a great way of showing you can combine text and images or text and numbers in your presentation. Your number information can be presented in the form of charts and graphs to help support points made in the text.

You may be able to get hold of a marketing strategy form the Internet. This gives you a chance to look at how information is presented; if you think it is particularly effective, you may be able to use your IT skills to create a similar structure and turn it into a template for your own work. This means you will generate evidence that you can develop the structure of your presentation, one aspect of the key skill requirement on presenting information.

Finance

Regardless of how finance is assessed in the GNVQ, there will still be an opportunity to use IT. You might be able to access company financial information using the Internet to help you become more familiar with finances and better prepared for what might come up in the assessment. Finance covers how to construct simple accounts, balance sheets and profit and loss accounts, and this will give you opportunities to develop information by using spreadsheets or financial software. You might be able to use the Internet to find financial information and annual reports that help you determine financial ratios like return on capital employed, profit margin ratios, asset and stock turnover, current and acid test ratios.

Though you might not be preparing information as evidence for your portfolio (perhaps the unit is externally tested), you could be using IT to help you calculate this information and to understand relevant concepts when you come to revise them. This means instead of your purpose being to create a report for your business portfolio, your purpose is to present information as clear notes that use text and numbers to help you revise how to interpret financial information and construct accounts.

Preparing revision notes using IT would be one way to generate evidence. Producing revision notes is your purpose and you would be the audience.

You need to take extra care that the numbers, graphs and text are very clear and everything is correctly explained. Ask your teacher to check your drafts for accuracy and ask your classmates how clear they find your explanations; this will be an important and useful way to ensure your notes make good revision material.

You can also generate evidence to show you can plan and select information; maybe research the performance of a public limited company and obtain information on share prices, dividends and price/earnings ratio.

Business planning

The clearest opportunity to generate IT evidence in this type of unit is when looking at financial planning. The unit evidence requirements may even ask for an IT spreadsheet or similar IT format. IT can help you find appropriate information if you want to base your financial plan on market analysis and also help with presenting budgets, break-even analysis, cash flow forecasts and projected profit and loss; it can be used to create a start-up balance sheet.

You will also be able to generate evidence for planning and selecting information, if you take advantage of IT to help you find and use primary and secondary market research data and competition analysis for your market report.

You might be able to use commercially produced business planning software. Banks and building societies sometimes provide helpful software. There may also be help with business planning on the Internet. By making appropriate and effective searches for this type of information, you will also be generating evidence for the key skill requirement on planning and selecting.

Make sure you integrate text and graphics in your business plan. This will produce a more dynamic, more interesting and more readable document and it will help you to meet the IT evidence requirements much more easily.

Businesses at work

Look for opportunities to work with and analyse the impact that information and communication technology has on the internal and external communications of a business. Depending on the nature of your study, you may also be able to analyse how Internet and online technology influence the way the company does business and presents itself to potential customers.

What you must know
Part 1: The Learning Curve will help you with the knowledge you need.

What you must do
Part 2: The Bottom Line will help you with the evidence you need.

Construction and the Built Environment Vocational A-level

About the specifications
The Construction and Built Environment awards study towns and cities that make up the environment, including their buildings and their civil engineering infrastructure. They also look at the technology and performance of structures, buildings and services within buildings, such as water and energy supplies. Common to all these studies are the ideas of investigating, surveying, measuring, design and reporting results. Optional units cover architecture and design, building, civil engineering, building services engineering, town planning and development.

Topic areas
Investigating the environment
Evaluations and surveys
Design procedures
Performance of materials, structures and services

Planning and selecting information
The investigation of environments, on the scale of a town or a building or in the detail of building services, provides many opportunity for using IT. You need to break the proposed activity into a number of tasks and the following activities will produce the evidence you need:

- Using the Internet to find and select background information about environmental issues, town features and other topics of investigations.
- Selecting and interpreting maps, plans and technical drawings in electronic formats.
- Making observations and measurements using electronic equipment.
- Finding and selecting electronic data on populations, economies and other aspects of towns and regions.

Check out the **websites** listed on page 122.

The processes for designing towns, structures, buildings and services require you to plan your activities and interpret many sources. Design decisions are also informed by technical knowledge on particular materials or technology. Here are some typical IT activities:

- Finding background information relevant to client requirements
- Selecting and interpreting maps, plans and technical drawings in electronic formats
- Using online and offline databases to find and select data about materials and components
- Selecting information from your own readings and surveys

Remember to keep evidence to show that you sometimes had a choice of search methods and information sources, such as different Internet sites, and indicate why you made a particular selection. Be able to compare the advantages and limitations of your methods and information.

Developing information

To use your field observations, your measurements and any other data you have collected, you will need to assemble it in documents with consistent and logical formats, e.g. tables and spreadsheet grids. You will be able to show how you explore and develop the information when you do calculations, find trends and produce graphics. Here are some possible activities connected to the key skills unit:

- Assembling sets of field readings and obtaining statistical results
- Developing design drawings using CAD
- Developing statistical results from large data sets, e.g. population trends, component performances
- Calculating areas for plots of land, roads, sections through hills, buildings, components, etc.
- Calculating volumes of earth mounds or trenches, buildings, rooms, pipes, ducts, etc.
- Calculating energy use in buildings

When exploring and developing your data, you need to show how you tried different values or rules; you can generate evidence by keeping a few spreadsheet printouts that did not give good results. As part of your activities you also need to exchange information by using email or sharing electronic documents.

Presenting information

You need to use IT to present your results in an effective manner and you need to show evidence of how you developed your presentation. Investigations in construction and the built environment offer good IT opportunities to present findings using text, images and numbers in a variety of formats. Here are some typical activities:

- Presenting information about towns, structures, construction details and service installations
- Showing details of design using drawings, visualisations and other graphics
- Giving slide presentations to explain design options and final choices
- Presenting statistical data, trends and other results using charts and graphs
- Presenting the results of energy-use calculations

As you develop your presentation you should keep some earlier drafts to show how it has altered; perhaps you've improved the layouts. It is useful to ask other people to give you feedback on your drafts and possible presentation methods; the key skill unit requires that your final presentation should suit its audience. The presentation needs to be technically correct and it also needs to make sense, so check it carefully and give it a proof-read.

What you must know
Part 1: The Learning Curve will help you with the knowledge you need.

What you must do
Part 2: The Bottom Line will help you with the evidence you need.

EVIDENCE FROM VOCATIONAL A-LEVEL COURSES | 93

Further opportunities for evidence

Projects for town development and construction involve many aspects of finance, such as mechanisms for raising money, estimating costs and tracking the flow of money. Some optional units in Construction and the Built Environment include analysis of financial aspects which provide good evidence for the key skill. Construction firms are among the larger companies listed on the stock market, and tracking and analysing their performance is another opportunity to use the Internet and spreadsheets.

Engineering Vocational A-level

About the specifications
The Engineering awards study engineering organisations in terms of business, finance, the economy and the environment. They also include units that apply principles of design, materials technology, science and mathematics. Optional units cover electrical engineering, mechanical engineering, telecommunications and automotive engineering.

See also: **Design and Technology A-level**, page 70.

Topic area 1
Investigating engineering organisations

Planning and selecting information
In carrying out case studies of an engineering organisation, you will need to find written, numerical and graphical data of various types relating to its engineering activities and you will need to investigate the various relationships and links within the organisation. By using databases, such as the Internet, you will also be generating evidence for the key skills unit.

You will need to plan what aspect of production or service you are going to study and select appropriate data for calculation and presentation. Remember to keep evidence to show that you sometimes had a choice of search methods and information sources, such as different Internet sites, and try to indicate why you made a particular selection. Be able to compare the advantages and limitations of your methods and your information.

Developing information
To use your data you will need to assemble it in documents with consistent and logical formats, e.g. tables and spreadsheet. You will be able to show how you explore and develop the information when you do calculations, find trends and produce graphics. Here are some possible activities connected to the key skills unit:

- Analysing company accounts and statistical data associated with the local economy and the national economy.
- Converting information to quantities, percentages and other relevant comparisons.

- Financial decisions on an aspect of production or service provision; record any relevant calculations.
- Using financial formulas to calculate costs, profits, return on capital, etc.

When exploring and developing your data you need to show how you tried different values or rules; you can generate evidence by keeping a few spreadsheet printouts that did not give good results. As part of your activities you also need to exchange information by using IT methods such as email.

Presenting information

The results of your investigations into various aspects of an engineering organisations will require a variety of IT techniques to interpret and present them. Here are some opportunities:

- Structure and functions of an organisation
- Links between engineering activities and commercial activities
- Information flow between parts of an organisation

Check out the **websites** listed on page 123.

As you develop your presentation you should keep some earlier drafts to show how it has altered; perhaps you've improved the layouts. It is useful to ask other people to give you feedback on your drafts and possible presentation methods; the key skill unit requires that your final presentation should suit its audience. The presentation needs to be technically correct and it also needs to make sense, so check it carefully and give it a proofread.

Topic areas 2
Performance and design of engineering products
Performance and design of engineering services

Planning and selecting information

Several units investigate the performance and design of chosen engineering products or services. You will therefore have opportunities to use IT techniques in the following activities:

- Using online and offline databases to find and select data about materials and components
- Finding technical and marketing data from manufacturers and suppliers to assist practical investigations of new technology
- Interpreting information taken from a design brief and the related drawings
- Selecting information from your own measurements such as from a mechanical engineering product

You need to plan efficient techniques for getting the information and be able to select useful information. Remember to keep evidence to show that you sometimes had a choice of search methods and information sources, such as different Internet sites.

EVIDENCE FROM VOCATIONAL A-LEVEL COURSES | **95**

Developing information

To use your measurements and your data, you need to assemble them in IT formats and then explore. Here are some examples:

- Assessing material properties and how they affect product performance
- Predicting energy values in electrical and mechanical applications
- Calculating quantities, dimensions and shapes for materials and components
- Calculating amounts and sizes

Presenting information

You will need to present the results of your investigations, and a good choice of IT techniques will help you illustrate findings, show trends and make comparisons. Here are some typical opportunities:

- Using graphs, charts, diagrams and CAD drawings
- Explaining mechanical and electrical features such as motion or energy efficiency
- Presenting the results of calculations and predictions
- Slide presentations explaining design options and final choices
- Presenting a final design solution accompanied by drawings and other graphics

You need to keep some earlier drafts as evidence that you have developed your presentation, you should seek feedback from other people to tailor it to your audience and you should give it a careful check.

What you must know
Part 1: The Learning Curve will help you with the knowledge you need.

What you must do
Part 2: The Bottom Line will help you with the evidence you need.

Health and Social Care Vocational A-level

About the specifications

The Health and Social Care awards study a range of topics; the compulsory units give you a broad understanding of some fundamentals and the optional units are slightly more specialised. Both optional and compulsory units can be used to generate key skill evidence. It is worth learning a little bit about all the units you are likely to study. This will allow you to get a better idea of how you can build up your portfolio of evidence for the information technology key skill, identifying which units can be used to generate evidence for the different key skill demands.

Here are some suggestions for how to use compulsory units to create key skill evidence. This information is designed to help you start planning and collecting the key skill evidence you need.

General opportunities for evidence

Whether you are taking physical measurements or collecting social research data, it is a good idea to learn how to use spreadsheets to store and manipulate your data. This helps you meet the requirement on creat-

Check out the **websites** listed on page 124.

ing and using structures and procedures for developing text, images and numbers, and it can also be integrated into your report writing.

The structures and procedures for developing texts, images and numbers will involve using spreadsheet software as you analyse and interpret numerical data and then generate graphs and charts. This is important; take time to learn it. It will generate evidence for your key skill but it will also improve the quality of your health and social care, and it will be a valuable asset in any future study.

Look for opportunities to use spreadsheets when studying topics like these:

- **Physical aspects of health**: when you record and work with measurements to determine the physiological status of individuals.
- **Research perspectives**: when you need to obtain and analyse primary and secondary data, using appropriate diagrams and charts.

You may also find specialist graphics packages that can help you show the results of any data you collect. This targets the key skill requirement to explore, develop and exchange information and derive new information.

Planning and selecting information

When you study topics like health, social care and early years services, you will find the Internet a useful source of information. It can take time to get information from local authorities and government agencies, so you may find it easier to have a look at their websites.

Take time to learn about appropriate database techniques and the use of Internet search engines. This will help you carry out effective searches or speed up your interrogation processes, and it is more likely to give you results that are useful.

You may find CD-ROMs a useful source of information on topics like anatomy, physiology and health. There are some good interactive and multimedia packages to help with this kind of topic. You should learn how to determine what makes for a successful and useful source of information and you should be able to discuss the merits of each package you come across. This will help you develop the ability to appreciate what makes for good IT packages. These skills will also help you gain key skill evidence in IT.

Remember you will need to ensure you are fully addressing the IT key skill requirements if you want to use your work as evidence. This means keeping relevant paper copies (use a screen dump or printout and keep relevant information). You will also need to show you can reflect on the advantages and limitations of your different sources of information, justifying any choices you made.

All this targets the key skill requirement to plan and use different sources to search for and select information.

Report writing

The IT key skill will encourage you to adopt a disciplined approach to keeping copies of your work, managing the various versions of your work

EVIDENCE FROM VOCATIONAL A-LEVEL COURSES | 97

to avoid losing it, and it will encourage you to use spellcheckers and grammar checkers on your work. All this will help to improve the quality of your vocational work.

Learning to make effective use of IT for planning research, selecting information and developing presentations may also give you greater confidence in your work and help you meet some vocational grading requirements.

Producing a research project on a topical issue related to health and social care or early years provision constitutes the substantial issue asked for in the key skill specifications; it allows you to generate evidence for all three requirements.

Health and social care issues

The Health and Social Care Vocational A-level tends to ask for portfolio evidence to be given in the form of an investigation or a report. When the specifications ask for an investigation they usually expect you to write a report. However, you may be able to give your evidence in the form of a presentation. Either way, the IT key skill can help you to produce a good quality piece of work on computer. You will also be able to use this evidence for your IT key skill.

IT focus

Very often units will ask you to comment on, acknowledge or follow appropriate ethical codes or to discuss issues related to ethics and client confidentiality. This is an important aspect of the IT key skill. You may be able to discuss the particular issues related to using IT in aspects of health and social care.

What you must know
Part 1: The Learning Curve will help you with the knowledge you need.

What you must do
Part 2: The Bottom Line will help you with the evidence you need.

Hospitality and Catering Vocational A-level

About the specifications

The Hospitality and Catering awards study a range of topics; the compulsory units give you a broad understanding of some fundamentals and the optional units are slightly more specialised. Both optional and compulsory units can be used to generate key skill evidence. It is worth learning a little bit about all the units you are likely to study. This will allow you to get a better idea of how you can build up your portfolio of evidence for the information technology key skill, identifying which units can be used to generate evidence for the different key skill demands.

Here are some suggestions for how to use compulsory units to create key skill evidence. This information is designed to help you start planning and collecting the information technology key skill evidence you need. However, there are more general opportunities as well.

Topic areas

There will be three main areas to consider when you generate evidence:

- Producing your vocational evidence

- Research and collecting material
- Specific hospitality and catering opportunities

Vocational evidence

Vocational evidence is what you need to generate for your course. Here we are focusing on developing information and presenting information. By producing your final assessments using IT, you will be able to target these specific parts of the key skill while doing your vocational work. You will find that in trying to meet the key skill requirements, the general quality and presentation of your hospitality and catering work will also improve.

When you begin to use IT to produce your vocational evidence, you will have an opportunity to integrate text and graphics in the reports you do for your vocational assessments. Depending on the topic, you may be able to integrate tables of statistics, measurements or quantities.

Any areas of the course will involve some research or investigation and a variety of information. There will be opportunities to develop and refine the presentation of texts, images and numbers and improve the impact of your work by changing formats or layouts. This allows you to adapt your work to make it more accessible to different audiences.

Research and collecting material

This area targets the planning and selecting information aspect of the key skill. The Internet can be very useful when finding out aspects of the industry. Many hospitality and catering service providers are likely to have some form of presence on the Internet. They might have their own website or they may feature in work done by other people.

The Internet is always a useful port of call when starting out your research, and by developing search and interrogation skills you will access the information you need more effectively. These skills will stop you getting bogged down with unnecessary information and they will help you develop appropriate key skill evidence.

CD-ROMs may also be a useful source of information, allowing you to show that you can use different sources to search for and select information required for different purposes. The key skill also asks you to reflect on the advantages and limitations of different sources of information, so keep this in mind when you are using the CD-ROMs or the Internet. You can use the results of successful searches for your vocational work and to show that you can make effective use of the technology for the key skill. You will also be able to discuss what you thought of the technology and this will generate additional evidence for the key skill.

You may also find specialist graph packages that can help you show the results of any data you have collected. This targets the key skill requirement to explore, develop and exchange information and derive new information.

Hospitality and catering opportunities

This area is likely to involve all aspects of the IT key skill and could be used to create evidence for one substantial activity that includes tasks for all three areas.

You will find there is a link between how the IT key skill is asking you to think about the area of new technology and how the industry is reacting to it. You are asked to consider the potential for information technology and to show that you can use it effectively. The hospitality and catering industry is beginning to exploit the potential of information technology in wider areas and is going through similar experimentation and thought processes.

Hospitality and catering has long used IT applications for finance, purchasing and stock control. However, the Internet and other developments have created a host of new opportunities and the industry is beginning to exploit them. For example the Internet and online technology have meant changes to marketing and booking.

One interesting area of IT is the potential to present similar information to different audiences in different ways. For example, a menu card can be designed to appeal to children, or it can be targeted at different groups of adults. Theme outlets can use IT to help create the appropriate concept presentation.

What you must know
Part 1: The Learning Curve will help you with the knowledge you need.

What you must do
Part 2: The Bottom Line will help you with the evidence you need.

Information and Communication Technology Vocational A-level

About the specifications

The Information Technology awards study and apply different methods of representing and processing numbers in computers. There are also opportunities to work with data communications, networks, operating systems and a range of hardware and software.

As you are already doing a course in information technology, it may seem easy and logical to gain the key skills unit in information technology. So it is, but you need to remember that the key skill is about *using* information technology to help you meet your aims or goals, not IT in isolation. It is not enough merely to find and present information using IT; you need to have a purpose for using the information you collect.

Providing evidence

You also need to provide evidence that you can apply your information technology skills, at the correct level, in the following three areas:

- Planning and selecting information
- Developing information
- Presenting information

See also: **Computing A-level**, page 69.

Part 2 of the book explains the requirements for evidence and suggests how you might capture evidence for each area. Level 3 also requires that you plan and carry out at least one substantial task using IT. You should therefore look at your course work or projects as a major opportunity to generate evidence.

Land and Environment Vocational A-level

About the specifications

The Land and Environment awards study a range of topics; the compulsory units give you a broad understanding of some fundamentals and the optional units are slightly more specialised. For example, you may choose to take units more concerned with plant or animal management. Both optional and compulsory units can be used to generate key skill evidence. It is worth learning a little bit about all the units you are likely to study. This will allow you to get a better idea of how you can build up your portfolio of evidence for the information technology key skill, identifying which units can be used to generate evidence for the different key skill demands.

Here are some suggestions for how to use compulsory units to create key skill evidence. This information is designed to help you start planning and collecting the key skill evidence you need. However, there are more general opportunities as well.

General opportunities for evidence

Consider producing your report-based evidence on computer. A quick look through the evidence requirements for the compulsory units will reveal a range of different opportunities to present information involving text, numbers and images. This will help you meet the requirements on presenting information. Make sure your work is clear and accurate and check that it meets your purpose and the needs of the audience (the reader). All this will help ensure your Land and Environment work is effectively presented. This will benefit you in meeting the Land and Environment requirements and may also help you meet some of the requirements for higher grades.

Specific opportunities for evidence

Environmental analysis

This topic would constitute a substantial activity that could be used to generate evidence for the three IT key skill areas. You will certainly need to plan how to do this type of activity, breaking it down into a series of smaller tasks. You might need to collect information about relevant organisations and you may be able to find some help or information on company websites.

Having collected the necessary information you will have a chance to show you can select the most appropriate items using relevance and quality as your criteria. It is worthwhile doing a little surfing on the Internet to see what information is available for environmental impact analysis. You can also show you have used some conditional searches, e.g. using AND.

Try to collect important numerical data then use your IT skills to develop it and perhaps derive new information. If you come across large amounts of numerical data during your searches, use spreadsheet technology to help you organise and deal with it if this is appropriate.

You should consider using images to help get points across in your report. Scanned photographs or images from the Internet can help make your work come to life and they set the business in a clear environmental context. Using images helps to generate further evidence that you can develop and present information.

Monitoring and managing ecosystems

Look for opportunities using IT to help you collect, organise and work on any primary data collected as a result of the practical survey work you do. You might be able to represent numbers of species and frequency on graphs generated by spreadsheets. You may also be able to create diagrams and use graphics to support explanations of how the ecosystem works. You could consider scanning in maps of the location and use them to mark up diversity and distribution based on your recorded data. The vocational evidence may even ask you to use simple and easily understood ways of presenting your survey results.

The requirement on presenting information encourages you to develop organisational discipline and to spend time thinking about how information should be presented; these skills will be particularly useful in helping you sort out the evidence for this topic. You will find it a useful way to organise and present your Land and Environment work that may contain a mix of text, statistics and even images like photographs or maps. The key skill could be a useful tool in helping to ensure you present your work effectively and clearly, organising it in a logical manner.

Check out the **websites** listed on page 121.

Further opportunities for evidence

Land and Environment	IT evidence
Investigating the sector	*Databases and Internet:* for investigating the contribution of business to the UK economy
	Word processing and desktop publishing: for report writing and bringing wide-ranging evidence requirements together in a logical structure
	Presentation software: helpful in ensuring you explain the features of the organisation
Animal management	*Spreadsheets:* recording research results of dietary needs and consumption. Analysing the data and producing graphs
Natural resources	*Spreadsheets and graphics software:* for data recording, data analysis, graphs and charts explaining and showing features of the environment and business organisations
Managing ecosystems	*Spreadsheets and graphics software:* recording survey results, producing statistics with appropriate calculations and graphs

What you must know
Part 1: The Learning Curve will help you with the knowledge you need.

What you must do
Part 2: The Bottom Line will help you with the evidence you need.

Leisure and Recreation Vocational A-levels

About the specifications
The Leisure and Recreation awards study a range of topics; the compulsory units give you a broad understanding of some fundamentals and the optional units are slightly more specialised. Both types of units can be used to generate key skill evidence. It is worth learning a little bit about all the units you are likely to study. This will allow you to get a better idea of how you can build up your portfolio of evidence for the information technology key skill, identifying which units can be used to generate evidence for the different key skill demands. The information below is designed to help you start planning and collecting evidence for the IT key skill unit.

Planning and selecting information

Investigating leisure and recreation
Investigation into the UK leisure and recreation industry constitutes a substantial activity that you could use to generate IT evidence for the three different IT requirements (planning, developing and presenting information). Collecting information for this topic will involve all aspects of the key skill. As you try to establish the scale and significance of the industry, its structure and its key components you will have an opportunity to use the Internet and demonstrate your ability to carry out effective searches.

The nature of the unit means you are likely to generate lots of information using Internet searches. You will have plenty of opportunities to show you can narrow your searches to generate useful information. You will also have plenty of opportunities to judge this information and select it in terms of its quality and usefulness to your purpose.

The sports industry
The Internet is a good starting point as you investigate your two chosen sports. You may find that the Internet opens up the opportunity to look at one UK sport and contrast it with a sport in another country. For example, you may find that sports in the USA seem very different in how they are organised and sponsored. Basketball, American football, ice hockey and baseball all have team and national websites. You will certainly get a clear impression of the money and importance for the mass media. Regardless of your chosen sport, you will have the chance to show you can carry out effective searches and make decisions about the information you collect.

Developing information

The sports industry
There will be several statistics that can be collected and developed using IT. You may have to explain the scale and economic importance of your chosen sports in terms of the numbers employed, the numbers of partici-

See also: **Travel and Tourism Vocational A-level**, page 115.

pants and the financial turnover. This might be your chance (a) to create and use structures and procedures for developing numbers by sorting and grouping the information and (b) to analyse and interpret numerical data using spreadsheet software. Having the appropriate figures available will mean having an opportunity to create graphs and charts using IT to help illustrate main points in your text. Having this type of number information available will certainly allow you to reach and justify your own conclusions, thus creating new information.

Leisure and recreation in action
You may have an opportunity to explore ways of developing financial information using IT. You may even want to try and explore basic project management techniques using IT. Help others to understand your business objectives and your resource needs by finding ways to express your figures using graphs and charts rather than using statistics. Pie charts can be a useful way of showing how your resource needs are divided; they can be generated using spreadsheet software.

Investigating leisure and recreation
There will be an opportunity to use spreadsheets and graph techniques when describing the scale of the industry and its economic importance to the UK. Check your numbers as you enter them; this will be one way of using relevant data and using it accurately.

Presenting information

The sports industry
The requirement that you present your work in a logical and well-structured format is an open invitation to use IT. You will find that in producing your vocational evidence, you will be able to use IT to help combine text and graphics. There will be an opportunity to use graphs to show major trends in each of your sports and to explain the economic and financial statistics. The following key skill requirements can all be met:

- Developing the structure of your presentation
- Developing the presentation of text and numbers
- Meeting your purpose and satisfying your reader
- Presenting accurate information
- Checking and refining your work
- Using appropriate spelling, grammar and punctuation

Leisure and recreation in action
You can generate IT evidence by producing your business plan using a computer. Make sure you include ways of presenting your numbers. You can achieve effective team involvement by having regular team meetings with clear agendas and minutes that record appropriate discussion and decision making. Word processing templates are available for creating agendas. These templates could be customised for your particular group

---

Check out the **websites** listed on page 121.

What you must know
Part 1: The Learning Curve will help you with the knowledge you need.

What you must do
Part 2: The Bottom Line will help you with the evidence you need.

needs; they represent another way of using IT and presenting important team decision making and information.

Investigating leisure and recreation
Word processing templates can help you to create your own CV (sometimes called a resume); you can also customise them. Customising a template will generate evidence for the requirement on presenting information.

Manufacturing Vocational A-level

About the specifications
The Manufacturing awards study a range of topics; the compulsory units give you a broad understanding of some fundamentals and the optional units are slightly more specialised. The optional units include chemical production, engineering manufacturing and a more business-oriented approach to manufacturing. Both types of units can be used to generate key skill evidence.

Here are some suggestions for how to use compulsory units to create key skill evidence. This information is designed to help you start planning and collecting the key skill evidence you need. However, there are more general opportunities as well.

General manufacturing opportunities

A great deal of the manufacturing evidence asked for in the Vocational A-level will be in the form of written evidence. Given the type of content you will be working with, you should find plenty of chances to generate evidence of developing information and presenting information. By producing your final evidence for manufacturing on computer and striving to meet the IT requirements for presenting information, you will not only generate key skill evidence but also improve the quality of your vocational evidence. Meeting the key skill requirements will ensure your work is properly organised, meets your intended purpose, is clear and reader friendly, and has been checked for appropriate spelling, grammar and punctuation. This may give you a better chance of meeting the grading requirements.

Using IT also makes it easier to produce draft copies for others to comment on. Make sure you are fully aware of any requirements before you start the vocational work; this will help you to generate evidence for your Manufacturing Vocational A-level and your IT key skill.

There will also be a number of opportunities to carry out research and investigations into different areas of manufacturing. These will provide you with opportunities to access information from the Internet and CD-ROMs. By doing this effectively, you will improve the quality of your vocational work and you will generate evidence for the key skill. This targets the requirement on planning and selecting information. Whenever

EVIDENCE FROM VOCATIONAL A-LEVEL COURSES | 105

you are collecting information and dealing with figures there is a chance to generate graphs and charts using IT.

IT has a significant role to play in most aspects of manufacturing and as a result you will find there will be some opportunity to generate at least a little IT evidence in the various subjects you study. When you work on your vocational evidence, perhaps using CAD, you will have an opportunity to reflect on how it is done in industry. This will allow you to generate evidence showing that you can compare your use of IT with systems used elsewhere. When looking at health and safety issues and any environmental impacts of manufacturing, you can also consider how to work safely with information technology and how to minimise its health risks.

Specific manufacturing opportunities

Developing a design
When you are working on a design portfolio, you might be asked to collect market research information, perhaps entering results into spreadsheets. This type of data can often be represented using graphs, tables and charts, so you may have opportunities to work on developing information. In particular, you could be learning how to create and use structures and procedures for developing texts, images and numbers.

Once you have developed the information from the market research results, you can write it up as a report and concentrate on generating evidence for the requirements on presenting information. If you are producing your design portfolio for a client, you have a specific audience and purpose to target and a reason to ensure your work is accurate and makes sense. (The teacher could play the role of client.)

> Check out the **websites** listed on page 123.

Presenting a design
A variety of IT techniques are used to present design proposals. Much of the emphasis could be on work in two or three dimensions. Therefore, the vocational work will probably require you to show some ability in:

- Using computer-aided design (CAD)
- Producing 3D graphics and visualisation
- Presenting images
- Producing flow diagrams and schematics
- Using desktop publishing (DTP)
- Using computer presentation packages

These activities will provide you with opportunities to work on manufacturing and key skills evidence simultaneously, but do not neglect the key skill requirements as you work towards your Vocational A-level.

The world of manufacturing
When studying the world of manufacturing, you will probably need to interpret statistical information about gross domestic product (GDP), sector trade balances and numbers employed in the manufacturing sector, or even numbers employed by the local industry. This should provide

opportunities to meet some of the requirements on presenting information as well as opportunities to generate graphs and charts.

You will also be able to meet some of the planning and selecting information as you look for and choose appropriate information using Internet search engines, CD-ROMs, etc. You could check the websites of organisations that represent different aspects of manufacturing, like the Confederation of British Industry and the Engineering Employers Federation. You could also look at websites for specific companies.

Further opportunities for evidence

Manufacturing areas	IT opportunities
Production, planning and costing	Databases of production information Spreadsheets to cost different options Project management software to help planning
Business organisation and departmental communications	Email, shared-access documents like databases and project plans

What you must know
Part 1: The Learning Curve will help you with the knowledge you need.

What you must do
Part 2: The Bottom Line will help you with the evidence you need.

Media: Communication and Production Vocational A-level

About the specifications

The Media awards study a range of topics; the compulsory units give you a broad understanding of some fundamentals and the optional units are slightly more specialised. You may choose optional units that concentrate on print, audio or video media. Both types of units can be used to generate key skill evidence. It is worth learning a little bit about all the units you are likely to study. This will allow you to get a better idea of how you can build up your portfolio of evidence for the information technology key skill, identifying which units can be used to generate evidence for the different key skill demands.

Here are some suggestions for how to use compulsory units to create key skill evidence. This information is designed to help you start planning and collecting the key skill evidence you need.

Media products

Researching a proposal for a media artefact will give you opportunities to generate IT evidence. You may be required to use primary and secondary research methods to develop ideas for the media artefact, showing you can select appropriate sources of information, resources and research methods. This might be your chance to target the requirement on planning and selecting information.

The vocational demands follow the IT requirements quite closely, but you will have to spend a little time to pick up any additional requirements.

EVIDENCE FROM VOCATIONAL A-LEVEL COURSES | 107

For example, the key skill requires you to compare the limitations of different sources of information and to select items suitable for your purpose, but this is not a requirement of the Media awards. It asks only that you select the best information, resources and research methods. This may come out as a result of your IT work comparing the advantages and limitations of different sources of information.

Take time to think about IT in a media context. A coherent explanation of the strengths and weaknesses of the research may feature as part of the media grading criteria. By using the most appropriate IT sources, you can continue to generate evidence for your Media award and for the key skill requirement on planning and selecting information.

The Internet could be particularly useful for this unit. Using the Internet as a key source for your research will allow you to show you can use appropriate techniques for finding information and carrying out effective searches.

Marketing

When producing a marketing strategy for a new or existing media product you will find opportunities to generate evidence for planning and selecting information, developing information and presenting information. You could also use this as an opportunity to have one substantial activity that generates evidence for all three. Planning and producing a marketing strategy would constitute a substantial activity that could be broken down into a series of smaller tasks.

Planning and selecting information
You may have to collect evidence on audiences and competitors using primary and secondary research methods in order to inform and justify your marketing decisions contained in the marketing strategy. You may find that the Internet is a useful tool to help find the information you need. You could use IT to help you develop the research tools for primary research if you are planning to carry out a survey or create a questionnaire. This is worth considering because both methods will generate data that can be worked on using a computer, giving you a chance to meet the requirement on developing information.

Developing information
The main area worth exploring involves working on the data you collected using your primary research methods. You should consider entering data into spreadsheets and generate graphs to help illustrate and explain your findings. This will also allow you to derive new information as you evaluate your data to reach and justify conclusions from your findings. You may need to create other ways to enter and combine information in a consistent form, e.g. tables.

Presenting information
In this case your presentation is the final marketing strategy to be submitted as evidence for your media portfolio. Meeting the key skill require-

ments by developing the structure and content using the views of others to help improve your presentation, effective use of format and style to suit your purpose and checking accuracy and sense all will help you produce better quality evidence. This will help you to produce work that is will planned and organised; it may even lend a coherent and well-balanced approach to your marketing strategy, which might help with some of the vocational grading requirements.

Further opportunities for evidence

Depending on the available equipment, you could consider using computer technology to develop any moving-image media products you decide to create. Various software packages can be used, but there are three important things to keep in mind:

- Make sure you meet the vocational evidence requirements in full.
- Make sure you meet the IT key skills requirements.
- Avoid IT that goes beyond the requirements of the key skill.

Consider using IT to produce your revision notes. Suppose the unit on the workings of the media industry is to be externally assessed; a good set of revision notes would help you to prepare and you could produce them on a computer. In terms of the key skill requirements, your purpose is to produce revision notes and your audience is yourself.

By asking classmates to comment on the drafts, you could make sure your notes cover the right topics and explain the material clearly. Your teacher will also be a good person to check your work. You could develop graphs and charts using spreadsheets to help you understand patterns of IT ownership and employment. Graphs and charts can express patterns visually and may be easier to remember when you are tested.

What you must know
Part 1: The Learning Curve will help you with the knowledge you need.

What you must do
Part 2: The Bottom Line will help you with the evidence you need.

Performing Arts Vocational A-level

About the specifications
The Performing Arts awards study a range of topics; the compulsory units give you a broad understanding of some fundamentals and the optional units are slightly more specialised. Both types of units can be used to generate key skill evidence. It is worth learning a little bit about all the units you are likely to study. This will allow you to get a better idea of how you can build up your portfolio of evidence for the information technology key skill, identifying which units can be used to generate evidence for the different key skill demands.

Perhaps the best way to address the key skill requirements of the Performing Arts Vocational A-level is to focus on distinct areas of the key skill. But take time to look through the course requirements and plan how you will address the different requirements in the IT key skill. Remember that you need to find at least one occasion where you can carry out a substantial task that meets aspects of all three sections.

Planning and selecting information

- When studying historical and contemporary contexts you will need to carry out some research into different periods of history. You may need to do some digging to find out the artistic influences that have affected the style, content and presentation of the work you study. This might be a good opportunity to use CD-ROMs and the Internet.
- Web searches may reveal job and employment opportunities plus information on contracts or appropriate promotional materials.
- You might be required to research specific productions or you may wish to research a role you will play or a production you will stage. The Internet is a useful source of information.

Developing information

- Historical and contemporary topics may involve finding and presenting numerical data. Work on ways to present this data so it supports the accompanying text.
- Consider keeping an electronic diary of your performance projects. Record how the production develops and what you have been doing. Consider how best to lay out the diary, perhaps by using a template. You may find a ready-made template in your word processing package or perhaps on the Web.
- Having created your diary you can link it to other documents, perhaps a general calendar for the whole production; you could even link the document to a spreadsheet that documents the costs of the production. Creating this type of link between documents, experimenting and exploring ways to make them work effectively, all will help to generate evidence for the requirement on developing information.
- You might also want to consider having the team use an electronic calendar and a diary function, perhaps on an intranet. Software packages like Lotus Notes and Microsoft Outlook can create team calendars and diaries, and you will generate appropriate evidence as you learn how to set up and run an appropriate system for your team.
- One other possibility worth considering is to use specialist project management software to help you plan and schedule the production. If this software is available you could use it to plan the production identifying critical paths, key decision points and deadlines. This will help to generate a wealth of evidence for all aspects of the key skill.

Presenting information

- Consider using IT whenever you are asked to submit some form of written information or evidence. There may be few other opportunities to generate appropriate IT evidence in the Performing Arts GNVQ. You should also keep this in mind if you need to

produce promotional or marketing material. Promotion and marketing give you good opportunities to generate evidence because the purpose and the audience are clear.
- Working in teams can also be a useful opportunity as team meetings may require agendas, minutes, presentations, etc. Each can be produced on IT and again each has a very definite purpose and audience.
- Presentations can be made more dynamic and interesting using information technology, especially presentation packages. Start by satisfying the evidence requirements for Performing Arts then plan how you can generate IT evidence too.
- Consider using IT to produce your revision notes. Suppose the unit on the workings of the performing arts industry is to be externally assessed; a good set of revision notes would help you to prepare and you could produce them on a computer. In terms of the key skill requirements, your purpose is to produce revision notes and your audience is yourself. By asking classmates to comment on the drafts, you could make sure your notes cover the right topics and explain the material clearly. Ask your teacher to check them over too.
- You could develop graphs and charts using spreadsheets to help you understand patterns of performing arts funding and how the industry is divided into different sectors. Graphs and charts express patterns visually and may be easier to remember when you are tested.

What you must know
Part 1: The Learning Curve will help you with the knowledge you need.

What you must do
Part 2: The Bottom Line will help you with the evidence you need.

Retail and Distributive Services Vocational A-level

About the specifications
The Retail and Distributive Services awards study a range of topics; the compulsory units give you a broad understanding of some fundamentals and the optional units are slightly more specialised. Both types of units can be used to generate key skill evidence. It is worth learning a little bit about all the units you are likely to study. This will allow you to get a better idea of how you can build up your portfolio of evidence for the information technology key skill, identifying which units can be used to generate evidence for the different key skill demands.

A quick look at the evidence requirements for the Vocational A-level will show there are many opportunities to generate graphs and charts based on the information you need to find out, and many opportunities to combine the graphs with text to make interesting reports and studies. Take time to look at the potential opportunities for IT evidence within each of the units you do and begin to chart how you can build up your IT portfolio.

Here are some suggestions for how to use compulsory units to create key skill evidence. This information is designed to help you start planning and collecting the key skills evidence you need.

EVIDENCE FROM VOCATIONAL A-LEVEL COURSES | **111**

See also: **Business Studies A-level**, page 64; **Business Vocational A-level**, page 89; **Travel and Tourism Vocational A-level**, page 115.

Developments in retail and distributive services

Very often assessment evidence for this type of unit requires an extensive study illustrating current trends in retail and distributive services. The study can involve analysis of consumer behaviour, economic trends, changes in employment patterns and may also involve an analysis of your own local area, high street or mall. There are three points to keep in mind:

- Such an extensive investigation would represent a substantial activity that could generate evidence for all aspects of the key skill.
- The work will also provide opportunities to work with text, numbers and images. There will be plenty of opportunities to present statistics in tables or graphs, e.g. economic trends and employment patterns, and plenty of opportunities to use images, e.g. street maps and floor plans.
- IT can give you a way of holding all this work together and turning it into a coherent, well-organised and clearly presented study. This might also help you meet some of the grading requirements.

Check the websites of outlets in your chosen area. This type of research will give you evidence on searching and collecting. There might also be an opportunity to reflect on the growing importance of Internet sales and the potential changes this may bring to the way we shop and buy goods.

Finance

The growth in online share trading has made company information much more widely available. Carry out online searches to obtain financial data. Look in annual reports on company websites and explore other relevant sources.

Other websites may offer specific information on company profits and margins as well as share information. Check to see if any of the financial magazines and newspapers offer online facilities. You may find there are specialist advice and reference sites for help in understanding different financial terminology and concepts. These are all opportunities to meet the requirements on searching and selecting.

You may have an opportunity to work with specialist software that deals with finance and financial information like budgeting, forecasting and costing, balance sheets and profit and loss accounts. If not, consider using spreadsheet packages like Lotus 1–2–3 and Microsoft Excel.

The vocational evidence requirements may ask you to describe how financial data is recorded, stored and used or to explain techniques for budgeting, forecasting and costing, without actually producing any evidence to show you had a go at using relevant software. However, you might find that by exploring possibilities using some appropriate software you have the opportunity to gain a better understanding of the subject matter. This might help you produce better quality work and help you in meeting some of the grading requirements. You will also be generating evidence for the requirement on developing information.

Marketing

At the very least you will have an opportunity to present information containing text, images and even numbers. You could use information about a company's sales, turnover, profit and volume to create tables, charts or graphs. Setting information in context and showing yearly changes will provide further IT opportunities. Depending on the type of information you are given you may even be able to make predictions and show the expected outcomes in a diagram. Some specialist software has marketing and financial models you can run and test.

Merchandising

There might be the opportunity to make a presentation on merchandising. If you do a group presentation, consider using a software package like PowerPoint to help you. This will help you to make a more dynamic presentation and give you the opportunity to generate evidence for the requirement on presenting information. Presenting in this way gives you a definite purpose and clear audience needs to address.

When producing written work for your portfolio you may need to use sketches, diagrams or even photography to help explain how space is used in merchandising and display within specific organisations. This might give you an opportunity to show how you develop information as you explore ways to scan and incorporate images alongside your text.

What you must know
Part 1: The Learning Curve will help you with the knowledge you need.

What you must do
Part 2: The Bottom Line will help you with the evidence you need.

Science Vocational A-level

About the specifications
The Science awards investigate the types of science, organisations and people involved in the workplace and examine their links with the community and the economy. They also include units that increase your knowledge of particular scientific areas by carrying out practical investigations and linking the results to relevant industrial processes. Other units allow you to make extended scientific investigations into chosen areas of science or aspects of the scientific workplace.

Topic areas
Investigating the science workplace
Monitoring the activity of the human body
Controlling chemical processes
Controlling the transfer of energy
Synthesising organic and biochemical compounds

Planning and selecting information
One of your activities needs to be a substantial activity for which you plan your approach, breaking it into manageable tasks. Information technology is a natural tool for gathering scientific information and data; the key skill

See also: **Biology A-level**, page 61; **Chemistry A-level**, page 67; **Physics A-level**, page 83.

EVIDENCE FROM VOCATIONAL A-LEVEL COURSES

unit focuses on using IT to select the most useful information. Here are some activities to produce the evidence you need:

- Finding information about science-based companies
- Finding and selecting indicators of physiological status
- Finding and interpreting data about energy use in systems
- Finding and interpreting data related to chemical processes
- Selecting information from your own readings and surveys

Remember to keep evidence to show that you sometimes had a choice of search methods and information sources, such as different Internet sites, and indicate why you made a particular selection. Compare the advantages and limitations of your methods and your information.

Developing information

To use your information and numerical data, you will need to assemble it in documents with consistent and logical formats, e.g. tables and spreadsheet grids. The requirement to explore and develop the information should naturally arise from your need to do calculations, find trends and produce graphics. Here are some possible activities:

- Assembling physiological data sets and calculating statistics
- Establishing health norms for individuals
- Calculating rates of reaction, equilibrium constants and enthalpy changes
- Calculating the yields and results of volumetric analyses
- Calculating energy transfer and efficiency parameters
- Calculating fluid flow rates

When exploring your data you need to show how you tried different values or rules, so keep a few printouts that did not give good results. As part of your activities you also need to exchange information using IT methods, e.g. email.

Presenting information

You need to use IT to present your results in an effective manner and to show evidence of how you developed your presentation. Science investigations offer a good choice of IT opportunities to present findings using text, images and numbers in a variety of formats. Here are some typical activities:

- Gathering information on local organisations to show their structures and their types of work
- Comparing risk assessments relating to industrial or environmental applications of science
- Using charts and graphs to present statistical data, trends and other results
- Showing chemical calculations, e.g. rates of reaction, equilibrium constants and enthalpy changes
- Presenting the features of a system and its transfer of energy

Check out the **websites** listed on page 121.

- Describing compounds showing structures and nomenclature
- Explaining appropriate background knowledge, such as chemical and biochemical principles

Keep some earlier drafts to provide evidence that you have developed your presentation, perhaps with improved layouts. It is useful to ask other people to give you feedback on your drafts and possible presentation methods; the key skill unit requires that your final presentation should suit its audience. The presentation needs to be technically correct and it also needs to make sense, so check it carefully and give it a proof-read, especially any numerical data.

Further opportunities for evidence

Most scientific investigations provide good opportunities to collect evidence for the IT key skills unit. The key skills unit is organised into planning, developing and presentation, similar to an experiment or other scientific investigation. Investigations of organisations or processes may need analysis of costs or financial aspects. These activities can provide good evidence for the key skills unit by using the Internet and spreadsheets for tracking and analysing the stock market performance of technology companies.

What you must know
Part 1: The Learning Curve will help you with the knowledge you need.

What you must do
Part 2: The Bottom Line will help you with the evidence you need.

Travel and Tourism Vocational A-level

About the specifications
The Travel and Tourism awards study a range of topics; the compulsory units give you a broad understanding of some fundamentals and the optional units are slightly more specialised. All units can be used to generate evidence for the IT key skill. The information below is to help you start planning and collecting the evidence you need.

Investigating travel and tourism

Planning and selecting information
When collecting information on the UK travel and tourism industry, consider using CD-ROMs and the Internet. Then you can show you you compare the advantages and limitations of different sources of information, and you can show choose appropriate techniques for finding information. Become familiar with using Internet search engines; it will be an invaluable help in the future.

Developing information
You may need to generate graphs and charts to show the growth of the industry or its scale and significance to the UK economy. This will help

See also: **Geography A-level**, page 76.

EVIDENCE FROM VOCATIONAL A-LEVEL COURSES | 115

you with evidence on creating and using structures and procedures for developing text, images and numbers. Choose criteria that could be used to measure the growth of the industry in numbers. For example, the amount of people who holiday in the UK each year or the amount of revenue raised through UK tourism each year. This will help you to create charts and graphs that can be incorporated into your final report.

Presenting information

You will find that you can meet all the requirements in this aspect of the key skill if you turn your investigation of the travel and tourism industry into a written report using the computer. Concentrate of trying to use format, style and different techniques to enhance the impact of your work. Some word processing packages have a range of CV templates (sometimes called resumes). They also allow you to customise them to give your own particular style. Tailoring information for a particular purpose can be used to generate evidence for the requirements on presenting information.

Topic area 1
Customer service

There are two approaches to topics like customer service. The first approach relates to the experiences you have in customer service. The second approach relates to your evaluation of customer service in organisations generally. Both should help you generate evidence for the IT key skill unit. Look for the following opportunities to generate evidence.

Planning and selecting information

Look for opportunities to use IT when you are providing help or service to customers. If you are on a placement or simulated placement, try out the specialist systems used in the industry, otherwise use facilities like the Internet. When you are looking at the effectiveness of customer service delivery in travel and tourism organisations you may have the opportunity to comment on the significance and effectiveness of their different IT systems and software. This may help you collect evidence on comparing the advantages and limitations of different sources of information.

*Check out the **websites** listed on page 121.*

Developing information

If possible (and appropriate) try to get involved in communicating with others via email when you are involved in providing customer service to others. This might need you to be on a genuine placement, but a simulated work environment may suffice.

Presenting information

While the bulk of the opportunities come in producing your final report on customer service, there may also be some limited opportunities in your own practical experience. When working with others you might get the opportunity to use IT to help adapt a presentation so it meets the audience needs more effectively. You may also be able to comment on how the travel and tourism organisations you study present information in relation to the key skill requirements.

Topic area 2
Marketing

Planning and selecting information

Marketing uses information technology extensively and in a variety of ways. Many tourist organisations have their own websites. These can range from national organisations like the Scottish Tourist Board to smaller-scale ventures like the Melrose Traders. The Melrose Trader promote business in Melrose, a small town in the Scottish Borders. You are likely to find mission statements, objectives and information on the business environments when you look at the bigger organisations and sites. However, using smaller organisations and the information they provide may give you a better opportunity to create mission statements, objectives and an analysis of their environment.

This type of Internet use will give you a chance to show you can perform effective searches using relational operators to help you narrow them down. Having collected suitable information you will have plenty of opportunities to show you can select information that best suits your purpose. The range of information you collect will allow you to use quality as a criterion to help in making your judgements.

Presenting information

Some word processing templates may be particularly useful for travel and tourism. Brochure, newsletter and leaflet templates could be good for this type of evidence. Even if your evidence must be a report, you could illustrate your main points and suggestions by creating a brochure that actually demonstrates how well you understand the ways UK travel and tourism organisations use marketing. Invent a fictitious organisation and produce some marketing material for it.

What you must know
Part 1: The Learning Curve will help you with the knowledge you need.

What you must do
Part 2: The Bottom Line will help you with the evidence you need.

Information sources

See also: **Using the internet** page 16.

The following Internet websites can be useful starting points when searching for information. They are grouped in topic areas but there are many overlaps. Internet addresses can become outdated and you should aim to keep a list of favourites that are useful to you.

If you can't find the information you are looking for, you should use one of the search engines described in Part 1.

General

www.ngfl.gov.uk
National Grid for Learning
A useful portal to many sites education and learning sites in the UK

www.gsce.com
GCSE Answers
Offers practical help in GCSE English and mathematics, plus links to other websites.

www.bbc.co.uk/education
BBC Education
Includes useful information on many subjects and is a portal to a range of other websites.

babelfish.altavista.com
Translation website
Enter (or paste) your text and the website will translate to and from major languages.

www.learnfree.co.uk
Learnfree
A website for teachers, parents and learners, including useful tips about qualifications and studying.

English

www.ngfl.gov.uk
National Grid for Learning
A useful portal to many education and learning websites in the UK.

www.gsce.com
GCSE Answers
Offers practical help in GCSE English and mathematics, plus links to other websites.

www.plumbdesign.com/thesaurus
Visual Thesaurus
An interactive, animated thesaurus which displays related words on-screen and allows you to navigate connections between them.

daphne.palomar.edu/shakespeare
Shakespeare and the Internet
Timelines, biographical details and links to many other Shakespeare-related websites.

Mathematics

www.ngfl.gov.uk
National Grid for Learning
Useful portal to many education and learning websites in the UK.

www.gsce.com
GCSE Answers
Practical help in GCSE English and mathematics, plus links to other websites.

www.anglia.co.uk/education/mathsnet
Mathsnet
A variety of resources, including puzzles, tutorials, numeracy information and links to other maths websites.

www.nrich.maths.org.uk
Online Maths Club
Material for all ages and online answering service.

Science

www.wnet.org/savageearth
Savage Earth
Includes good introductions to plate tectonics, volcanoes, earthquakes and tsunamis (tidal waves). It has Flash animations and QuickTime movies and gives a useful overview without too many technicalities. Ideal for GCSE Science and useful for geology students.

www.bbc.co.uk/the_net/
BBC The Net
A magazine-style website on digital culture, including articles about the Internet and the issues surround it. Also provides links to some good web projects.

www.howstuffworks.com
How Stuff Works
Readable information to explain everyday technology and natural processes (such as car engines, combination locks, food, the immune system).

www.colorado.edu/physics/2000
Physics 2000
A journey through modern physics and its applications, with lots of interactive demonstrations and exercises. Materials geared to all levels and many wider topics, including health and food.

gslc.genetics.utah.edu
Genetic Science Learning Centre
This website provides genetic experiments which show how DNA, chromosomes and genes relate to conservation and forensic applications.

www.scicentral.com
SciCentral
Professional website which feeds news science stories to newspapers, TV and the Internet. See it here first. Includes an area designed to encourage science awareness among students.

Modern Languages

www.locuta.com
Centro Studi Italiani
A website specialising in Italian language learning. Has an electronic classroom area.

www.nene.ac.uk/lrs
Language resources
A University College Northampton website offering language resources for French, German, Italian and Spanish. Includes language learning, soundbites, quizzes, newspapers and links to other websites.

www.well.com
World Language Pages
A Liverpool John Moores University website offering a guide to language resources for many modern languages. It includes links to materials for language learning and suggestions about how best to use them.

Business

www.osl-ltd.co.uk
Oxford School of Learning
This website is designed for Business Studies at A level and has daily comprehension questions and essay plans on a wide range of topics. It has a number of Applied Business Studies questions too.

www.ft.com
Financial Times
The electronic version of the business newspaper. The website includes share prices, trends and currency conversion

www.economist.com
Economist
An online format of the popular business magazine which contains latest business news along with ideas, features, opinion and an analysis of international affairs.

www.oanda.com
Currency conversion
This website converts currency values and also contains a list of exchange rates for every day since 1990. Good for checking what your holiday money is worth before you go abroad and an excellent practical demonstration of currency conversion for maths students.

www.bized.ac.uk
Biz/ed
A website dedicated to business education with a huge pool of resources organised for UK qualifications and exams. Information includes data on 500 major companies, worksheets on the housing market, a virtual factor where A level and GNVQ business students can apply theory to a real-world business case.

www.bbc.co.uk/education/alvin/alvin.shtml
Investing for all
A BBC website designed for beginners. It contains FAQs (frequently asked questions), a 'jargon-buster' and a breakdown of what financial numbers mean.

Biology • Built Environment • Geography • Land and Environment • Leisure and Tourism

www.unfccc.de
Climate change
A United Nations website with useful beginner's guide to climate change, global warming and the ozone layer problem. The rest of the website contains in-depth information on all aspects of climate change.

www.nationalgeographic.com
National Geographic
Includes many interesting areas; a 'map machine' provides a choice of maps and views of anywhere in the world. Also includes information and tutorials on GIS.

www.scotese.com/earth.htm
Paleomap Project
A website devoted to the history of planet Earth, including detailed sequences of maps showing Earth over geological timescales. Good material for students studying continental drift in geography.

response.restoration.noaa.gov/kids/kids.htm
Environmental disasters
A US government website about the effects of oil spills or hazardous chemical accidents. Includes a guided tour to see how the experts deal with such environmental disasters, and simple experiments to investigate oil pollution and its effect on birds and animals.

www.countryside.gov.uk/what/f_forest.htm
Countryside agency
The website focuses on the new woodlands, community forests, on the edge of twelve major towns and cities. There is also information on National Parks, Areas of Outstanding Natural Beauty and walking trails for the countryside enthusiast.

www.terraquest.com
Virtual Antarctica
Use a virtual console to view images of Antarctica or learn about the ecology and wildlife of the region. Discover the history of Antarctic exploration and the environmental issues of the present.

www.ordsvy.gov.uk
The Ordnance Survey
A powerful geography resource for anything from local studies to contrasting localities and map-reading. The section on education includes aerial photography and wall maps.

www.schoolnet.ca/vp-pv/learning
Learning for a Sustainable Future
Activities cover air, biodiversity, habitat and infrastructure, production and consumption systems, social systems, soil, and water.

www.greatestplaces.org
The Greatest Places on Earth
Allows you to explore seven geographically different regions of the world. Includes sample video clips and soundbites which offer an insight into the culture and customs of the various countries.

www.the-education-site.com/emenu.html
Electricity
Contains information covering all of the main commercial power generation systems, including gas, coal, nuclear and wind.

Construction • Design and Technology • Engineering • Manufacturing

www.howstuffworks.com
How Stuff Works
Readable information to explain everyday technology and natural processes (such as car engines, combination locks, food, the immune system).

www.mmeade.com/cheat
Nutrition Cheat Sheet
A general interest website about food and health with information about vitamins, minerals and trace elements. There are summaries of what they do what happens if you don't get enough or too much, and recommended daily allowance (RDA).

www.innerauto.com
Autotour
A US website which examines the auto industry. You can see installation on videos and pictures and you can play an interactive game that lets you build your own car company.

www.ford.com
Ford Motor Company
The official website of the Ford Motor Company with information on its history and issues such as environmental policy. In addition to the specifications of current cars there are concept cars.

www.olen.com/food
Fast Food Facts
An interactive database that gives the nutritional values of different foods. The results include amounts of calories, fat, cholesterol, etc.

www.innerauto.com
Automotive Learning Online
This website has adopted a relatively simple approach to how a car and its moving parts work. The accompanying Java applets, along with clear descriptions of the function of individual components, make this an excellent starting point for the budding auto engineer, and for science and design and technology students.

Health and Social Care • Home Economics • Hospitality and Catering

www.nutrition.org.uk
British Nutrition Foundation
Food and nutrition information for consumers, design and technology students and teachers. There are useful GCSE and A level pages and a good list of other resources.

www.cre.gov.uk
Commission for Racial Equality
An excellent website on the work of the Campaign for Racial Equality. It covers racism and the law and it gives a list of FAQs.

www.bbc.co.uk/education/health/parenting/index.shtml
BBC Education – parenting
Contains common-sense advice for new parents on pregnancy, birth and child development. There are also facts on broader issues such as smoking during pregnancy and cot death.

www.open.gov.uk/doh/
Health of the Nation
A website from the Department of Health that covers national trends, including statistical data such as the percentage of children who smoke and the number of deaths through different types of cancer. A good source of health data with downloadable graphs, it includes details of national health targets.

www.olen.com/food
Fast Food Facts
An interactive database that gives the nutritional values of different foods. The results include amounts of calories, fat, cholesterol, etc.

www.thinkfast.co.uk/home.html
Thinkfast food website
Sponsored by the Health Education Authority, this website asks how can fast food be healthy? There is a quiz to test your knowledge and help you learn about the real properties of fast food and what it does to your body.

www.healthcalc.net
Healthcalc network
This website allows you to enter key data about your exercise level, diet, medical history and general health over a secure server, and find out how you shape up compared to the United States average.

www.wiredforhealth.gov.uk
Wired for Health
A government website which provides tailored health information and appropriate links to other websites. Topics include sun safety, smoking, physical activity, healthy eating, alcohol, accidents and mental health.

www.ama-assn.org
Atlas of the body
Includes good descriptions of the body and systems such as the respiratory system, the skeleton, the reproductive system and the endocrine system.

Index

A-level courses 57–85
   Art 58
   Art and Design Vocational 86
   Biology 61
   Business Studies 64
   Chemistry 67
   Computing 69
   Design and Technology 70
   General Studies 73
   Geography 76
   History 79
   Mathematics 80
   Physics 83
Art A-level 58
Art and Design Vocational A-level 86
assessment at level 3, external 55

Biology A-level 61
browsers 17
Built Environment Vocational A-level, Construction and the 92
Business Studies A-level 64
Business Vocational A-level 89

charts and graphs 25–6
checking and proof-reading 32
Chemistry A-level 67
collecting evidence 47–54
communicating 35
computer
   components 5
   interfaces 5–6
   parts 5
computer-aided design 34
Computing A-level 69
Construction and the Built Environment Vocational A-level 92
copyright 4

data protection 3–4
database
   output 14
   use 12
Design and Technology A-level 70
developing information 14

editing 6–7
email 35–8
Engineering Vocational A-level 94
evidence 44
   for level 3 46–54
   from A-level courses 58–85
   from Vocation A-level course 86–117
external assessment at level 3 55

file organization 8
finding and saving work 7–9
formats 29
formulas and spreadsheets 24

General Studies A-level 73

Geography A-level   76
glossary   40–42
GNVQ courses *see* Vocational A-level courses
graphics   33–9
graphs and charts   25–6

hardware and software   5
Health and Social Care Vocational A-level   96
History A-level   79
Hospitality and Catering Vocational A-level   98

ICT Vocational A-level   100
Information and Communication Technology Vocational A-level   100
information sources (websites)   118–25
Internet   16–21
    information sources   118
IT   2–3
IT Vocational A-level *see* ICT Vocational A-level

Land and Environment Vocational A-level   101
layout   29
Leisure and Recreation Vocational A-level   103
level 3   44, 46–54

macros   11
Manufacturing Vocational A-level   105
Mathematics A-level   80
Media: Communication and Production Vocational A-level   107

opportunities for generating evidence   57–117

organizing files   8–9
output from a database   14

paint packages   33
parts of a computer   5
parts of a database   12–13
Performing Arts Vocational A-level   109
Physics A-level   83
planning and selecting information   46
portfolio of evidence   45
presenting information   52
presenting work   38
printing   9–10
proof-reading and checking   32

Retail and Distributive Services Vocational A-level   111

saving and finding work   7–9
Science A-levels *see* Biology A-level; Chemistry A-level; Physics A-level
Science Vocational A-level   113
searching a database   15
searching and planning information   46
searching the Internet   19–21
software and hardware   5
sources of information   118–25
spreadsheets   22–6
    and formulas 24

templates   10–11
Travel and Tourism Vocational A-level   115

unit requirements   44–54
using a browser   17
using spreadsheets   22–4
using the Internet   16

Vocational A-level courses 86–117
- Art and Design 86
- Business 89
- Construction and the Built Environment 92
- Health and Social Care 96
- Hospitality and Catering 98
- Information and Communication Technology 100
- Land and Environment 101
- Leisure and Recreation Vocational A-level 103
- Manufacturing 105
- Media: Communication and Production 107
- Performing Arts 109
- Retail and Distributive Services 111
- Science 113
- Travel and Tourism 115

websites 16
   information sources 118–25
what you must do 44–54
word processors 27–32
world wide web 16
WYSIWYG 27